BIRMINGHAM

*The Building
of a City*

BIRMINGHAM

The Building of a City

Joseph McKenna

TEMPUS

For Fred Brown, Master Bricklayer (1913-1995)

First published 2005

Tempus Publishing Limited
The Mill, Brimscombe Port,
Stroud, Gloucestershire, GL5 2QG
www.tempus-publishing.com

British Library Cataloguing in Publication Data.
A catalogue record for this book is available from the British Library.

ISBN 0 7524 3489 6

Typesetting and origination by Tempus Publishing Limited
Printed in Great Britain

Contents

Introduction

In the two and a quarter centuries since William Hutton wrote his first history of Birmingham (1780), there have been no real attempts to explain the physical growth of the city itself. When did the significant developments take place and why? What influences formed the street plans we see today? Cities do not grow of their own accord, they are designed, financed and built by men. Cities develop because there is a need and it is people that create the need. This book explores the role of key figures in the development of Britain's second city and assesses the effect that their individual contributions made to the pattern of growth that today forms the built heritage of the city.

Landscape historian W.G. Hoskins recognised that, 'who built the needed houses, laid out the streets, financed the work, is still largely a mystery before the nineteenth century, above all in our provincial towns'. This challenge is now recognised as a proper and distinctive field of study. The town, for so long looked upon as a container of industry and men, is now assuming an importance in its own right. Studies of the interconnection between the growth of towns and the rise of industrialised society query the extent to which urbanisation itself may be regarded as an initiator, or a product, of economic growth. There is a need to explain how our towns were shaped and how the land was built on in the way that it was. The means by which the capacity of the town was increased involved the interlocking functions of landowners, developers, financiers and building craftsmen. To fully understand this we need to examine the extent to which the original owners or land developers surveyed the site, laid out the roads and provided amenities, whether land was conveyed freehold or leasehold and the extent to which builders were controlled by covenants. Financial factors too must be considered, such as the price of building land and the cost of preparing sites.

This book deals with the evolution of the landscape, of the city that is Birmingham. It is a landscape that was not transformed haphazardly, but rather with a degree of sophistication that until recently was considered to be the product of the late eighteenth century. Archaeology has shown us that this landscape is much older than we had thought. It was assumed that the Forest of Arden was the great barrier to the development of the region until the Anglo-Saxons arrived and cleared little pockets of land for their settlements. The reality now emerging is that the forest was not always there. During the Celtic and Romano-Celtic period, great swathes of the forest were cleared. Sites of human activity, homes and places of work, once situated within the former great forest, were discovered when the M6 Toll Road was constructed. Stone Age flint scatters from 8000 BC were discovered at Wishaw. At Sutton Coldfield an Iron Age settlement dating from 700 BC, the largest in the region, was discovered, which showed various phases of occupation. During the cutting of the M40 Birmingham-Oxford link, evidence of a Roman pottery operating on an industrial scale, with a considerable number of kilns, was discovered at Lapworth, right in the heart of what became the rejuvenated Forest of Arden. It was estimated that the pottery was probably supplying a region of some 20 miles around. As recently as June 2003, archaeologists discovered evidence of a Roman farm at Longdales Avenue, Kings Norton, on land being developed as a new cemetery. The dig found remains of timber buildings, ditches, pebble surfaces, a large barn and pottery dating back to the second century. This was a large developed site, situated in what was formerly forested land. Just as the forest grew back in the post-Roman period, the city itself has been rebuilt again and again. Studies of place-names are complicated: we know that certain places have changed their names, or incorporate much older Celtic names, as at Breedon Cross, Stirchley, which has elements of Celtic, Anglo-Saxon and Old English. Indeed Stirchley was originally called Streetly, indicating its Roman origins. Everything, it appears, is much older than we had suspected and people, by their very existence, have changed the landscape.

one

Landscape, Settlement
and Expansion

The Anglo-Saxon village of Birmingham was probably in existence before AD 650. The city's name is derived from the homestead (*ham*) of the people (*ing*) of Beorma. That we can be reasonably sure of the date is because Birmingham's name belongs to a group of place-names known as *ingaham,* which passed out of vogue before AD 700. The village of Birmingham was built on a sandstone ridge overlooking the river Rea, which acted as its eastern boundary. While the ridge itself was reasonably fertile and watered by natural springs, the land to the west, making up three quarters of what was to become the Manor of Birmingham, was poor agricultural land. In the Domesday book of 1086, there is a record of Birmingham's status at that time:

> *Richard holds of William* [Fitz Anculf] *four hides in Bermingcham. The arable employs six ploughs; one is in the demesne. There are five villains and four bordars with two ploughs. Wood*[land] *half a mile long and five furlongs broad. It was and is worth 20s. Ulwine held it freely in the time of King Edward* [1].

Aston manor was valued at £5, as was Handsworth, Northfield, and Yardley with Beoley. Sutton was valued at £4. Birmingham, with its ten recorded adults and valued at £1, was one of the poorest manors in the Midlands. The Domesday village of Birmingham would have existed around the village green that was eventually to become the Bull Ring. Long narrow strips of land radiating from the green had probably already been portioned out to the villagers, in what were later to become burgage plots. The green to the south would later be bounded by the parish church, dedicated to St Martin de Tours, while beyond this was the moated manor house of the deBirmingham family. A large proportion of the manor was retained by the family, in the form of parkland. Little Park, remembered today by Park Street, lay to the north-east of the present Bull Ring. Holme Park lay to the south-west, bordered by what was to become Smallbrook Street. Later, Rotton Park – a large hunting ground of some 600 acres which lay in the north-west quarter of the manor – was partially cut out of Birmingham Heath in the thirteenth or fourteenth century. To the north of Rotton Park lay the remaining square mile of wasteland that was Birmingham Heath, which reached up into, and included, a large stretch of Handsworth. This left perhaps just one-third of the manor for agricultural cultivation.

With little prospect of developing agriculturally, Birmingham's only hope of survival was to develop as a place of trade. In 1166 Peter deBermingham, also known as Peter FitzWilliam, lord of the manor and tenant of Gervase Paganel, Lord of Dudley, obtained a market charter from Henry II:

> *Henry King of England and Duke of Normandy and Aquitaine and Count of Anjou to Archbishops Bishops (Abbots) Earls Barons Justices Sheriffs Ministers and all his faithful men French and English of all England greetings. Know ye that I have given and granted to Peter Fitzwilliam the Sewer of Dudesley in fee and inheritance and to his heirs that he may have market on Thursday at his castle of Birmingeham with thol and theam and soc and sac and infangenethef and with all liberties and free customs. Wherefore I will and firmly command that the same Peter and his heirs shall have a market at his aforesaid Castle freely and quietly and honourably on the day aforesaid. Gervaise Paganel granted this same to him in my presence. Witness William Malet the Sewer John the Marshall William de Beauchamp Geoffrey de Ver Hugh de Perrers Walter de Dunstanvill. At Fekiha [2].*

This was the earliest market charter issued in Warwickshire and it gave Birmingham a lead over all its local rivals. The castle referred to in the charter was no more than a wooden stockade, surrounded by a moat, situated a short distance away from the present Bull Ring. In 1250 William deBermingham took the town's advancement a further step forward when he obtained a charter from Henry III granting him the right to hold a fair at his manor in Birmingham. The fair was to be held on the Eve of the Ascension and the following three days. Later that year the king granted a second charter permitting a second fair:

> *Whereas the King wills that a fair be held each year in his Manor of Birmingham. Now the Sheriff of Worcester is hereby ordered to proclaim through his bailiwick the holding of such a fair for three days, namely on the eve of the feast of St John the Baptist, on the day itself and the following day.*
>
> Given by the King at Winchester, the 6th November [3].

This fair was later transferred to Michaelmas, and the Ascension Day fair to Whitsun. The acquisition of both a market and fair charter provided the lord of the manor with a lucrative source of income from tolls and the rental of stallage, either by an annual payment, or a charge per foot of space.

Effigy of John deBirmingham: his family were prime movers in the expansion of the Norman town.

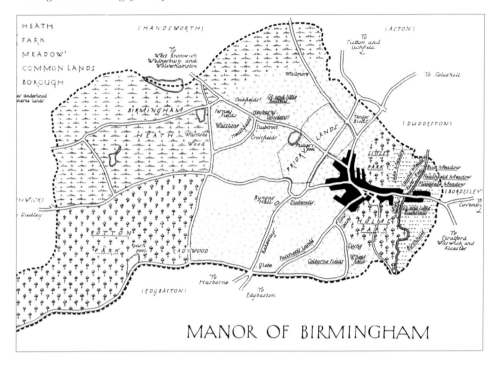

The Manor of Birmingham - a conjectural view.

The Moat, Birmingham, home of the deBirmingham family.

Contributing to Birmingham's growth, based on its market and fair charters, was its strategic position. The east-west routes through the Midlands tended to converge at convenient fords. The roads from Wednesbury, Dudley and Halesowen converged at Birmingham for the crossing of the Rea. To the east a similar convergence of west-bound routes from Coventry, Warwick and Stratford-upon-Avon also took place here. Routes north to south from Staffordshire to Warwickshire also used the river crossing, at Deritend. Recognising this importance, and by doing so it would attract travellers and tradesmen, the deBermingham family had a wooden, and later a stone, bridge erected here.

Markets and fairs promoted economic expansion, and as such provided an important contributory factor in the growth of a town. They attracted trade, and trade attracted people from the surrounding district. Sometimes they passed through the town as travellers, some came to trade, but increasingly they came to settle. The Lay Subsidy Roll of 1327 for Birmingham lists a number of incomers:

Jordan de Caldewell	John de Newehay
William de Neweport	Walter de Clodeshal
Henry de Caldewell	Thomas de Sleford
Elena de Hinkeleye	William de Hodenhull
Alice de Clodeshall	Thomas de Billeston
John de Coleshull	Eli de Illeleye
William de Wynesdon	William de Wodeston
Roger de Waleshale	

These men would have been Freemen, each holding, or leasing, a burgage tenement – that is a house plot – within the town, either around the original market square, or the extended High Street, or perhaps the newly constructed Edgbaston Street. As early as 1232, a group of Birmingham men had shown the way when they purchased their freedom from the feudal agricultural labour of summer hay-making [4]. This was a complete break with the past. The establishment of Birmingham as a borough, sometime before 1250, encouraged incomers, the town now being free from feudal obligations. Land became personal property within the manor. The idea that land, as it was under the feudal system, was a shared resource, was breaking down. This was the age of the individual, but individualism with a shared aim, that reached its fulfilment in the founding of the Guild of the Holy Cross. The Lay Subsidy Roll of 1332 suggests that eighteen of the sixty-nine taxpayers listed, or roughly one quarter, were recent arrivals. These would have been men with vision, who saw Birmingham as a place where they could prosper. This growth in population stimulated economic and urban expansion. By 1332 Birmingham possessed a parish church, a market and a priory dedicated to St Thomas. The priory, or Hospital of St Thomas, stood on the northern side of Bull Street until its dissolution in 1536. By deed of gifts the monks acquired an estate of some 100 acres in Birmingham and Aston. The priory park extended from the present Lancaster Street in the east to Easy Row in the west. The western part was laid out as a rabbit warren, or coningre (now Congreve Street).

During the fourteenth century, through the liberality of the more prosperous townsmen, a free chapel was established at the priory in Chapel Street (later renamed Bull Street) and a second, dedicated to St John, in Deritend. Two religious guilds were established, the Guild of the Holy Cross in New Street and the Guild of St John the Baptist in Deritend. Three chantries were founded, the first two by the Clodshale family, in the parish church, and the third, founded by Fulk Birmingham and Richard Spencer, at the altar of St Mary, in the priory.

Sometime before 1313, Birmingham received a severe setback to its expansion when it suffered what was described as a 'big fire'. Though there are no details, it would appear to have been very destructive. An account of the fire is recorded in the Court Rolls of Halesowen for 1313. One Thomas de Turkebi, who was trying to prove his status as a free man, revealed that the relative papers were 'burnt in the big fire of the town of Birmingham' [4]. That de Turkebi's word was accepted indicates that the fire must have been large for the inhabitants of Halesowen, situated some 6 miles away, to have been aware of it.

Rebuilding of the town appears to have commenced very soon afterwards. Town improvements also got underway, sponsored by local taxation. Money was raised for improvements to the town by imposing special market tolls for a limited period. The seventeenth-century Warwickshire historian, Sir William Dugdale, wrote:

> *In 12 Edward II* [1318]. *The inhabitants* [of Birmingham] *at the instance of Anomare de Valence Earl of Pembroke obtained a License to take Toll of all vendible commodities brought hither to be sold for the space of three years, viz., for every Quarter of corn a farthing &c., towards paving the town. But this work was not perfectly completed within that time nor of XV years after, for in 7 E 3,* [1333], *I find that they had another Pat: to take toll in like manner for the space of 3 more years* [5].

The Black Death of 1348-49 briefly saw a further check to expansion. There is evidence in the later Survey of Birmingham for 1553 that the manor was to some extent parcelled out anew, at this date, following ancient holdings falling into the de birmingham lord's hands. New tenancies were created by Fulk deBirmingham in Edgbaston Street and land at the junction of the present Smallbrook Street and Horse Fair. Recovery from the devastation of the plague was rapid, with craftsmen such as tanners, skinners, graziers, butchers, weavers, flax and yarn dressers, mercers and dealers taking up the vacant holdings. Further land, 80 to 100 crofts, was made available in the Forren; which is now the Ladywood district. New Street had also come into being by 1397, where in a deed of that year it is referred to as 'le New street', indicating its newness. Deritend, across the river in the Parish of Aston, also became part of the Borough of Birmingham as the town expanded eastwards. In 1381 Sir John deBirmyncham, 'lord of the villa or hamlet called Duryzatehende' and the parishioners of Deritend and Bordesley, successfully obtained an agreement from the prior and monks of the Priory of Tykeford, who possessed the parish

The old Bull Ring, heart of the medieval town. A conjectural view based on maps and views.

church of Aston, to be allowed to appoint their own chaplain to administer divine
services at the chapel lately built by themselves in Deritend.

By the Middle Ages Birmingham men were engaged in a number of economic
activities, including the wool trade, cloth making, leather working, pottery and metal
working. The town, and its market, were strategically placed at the centre of three
important woollen centres: the Welsh Marches, Lincolnshire and the Cotswolds.
Extensive sheep pens were constructed at the northern end of the High Street,
near the present Dale End, reaching up into lower Bull Street, which, because of
the large number of Welsh drovers using them, became known as Welch End. Many
Birmingham men acted as merchants in the wool trade. The most notable was
John atte Holte, of Edgbaston Street, who was a member of the Wool Merchants'
Assemblies, a national organisation, trading with the Continent. He is listed in the
Lay Subsidy Roll of 1332, as paying 10s 8d, the highest sum paid. A contemporary of
Holte's was Walter de Clodeshale de Birmyngham, who is referred to as one of the
leading wool merchants in Warwickshire in 1322 [6]. A third wool merchant, William
le Mercer, also appears on the Lay Subsidy lists.

Birmingham was ranked second only to Coventry among Warwickshire towns
marketing cloth by cloth makers such as Isabel le Webbe (1338), Richard le Webbe
(1339), John Smyth (1448-49), Nicholas Sherman, shearman, and John Snowedon,
dyer (1475). Tanning became established on the south side of Edgbaston Street,
and reaching down into Well Street or Digbeth; notable leather workers included

Thomas Phelip, saddler (1429), John Lorde, 'corbeserer' (1449), and John Smythe, skinner (1455). There was also a strong presence of Birmingham shoemakers in London for most of the fourteenth century. A pottery industry was established in Moor Street by the thirteenth century. Perhaps this accumulation of small industries, with its accompanying smoking kilns, could be described as an example of early industrial zoning, a degree of sophistication not usually associated with this period.

The tanning industry was being pushed out of the south side of Edgbaston Street by 1440, as the town expanded westward and land prices rose. In that year John Kockes leased a butcher's shop from owner Roger Cutte. It was situated between a shop owned by the Guild and a shop formerly owned by William Whichurch[7]. The street developed as a cheek-by-jowl mixture of private dwellings and shops.

The Guild of the Holy Cross came into being in 1392. Ostensibly a religious guild, it developed into a civic body whose works were carried out for the good of the whole town. A licence was granted to Thomas Sheldone, then dead, John Coleshulle, John Goldsmythe and William atte Slowe, burgesses of Birmingham, on 7 August 1392, enabling them to assign to the Master and Wardens of the Guild, eighteen houses, three tofts and six acres of land, the rent from which was to be used to pay for priests to celebrate Mass in the parish church, and perhaps more practically, to fund charitable works and look after the general welfare of the people of Birmingham. From a practical point of view, as the Commissioners of Edward VI later reported in 1553, the Guild established and maintained almshouses for the poor in Digbeth. They also maintained the parish clock and chime, and:

> *Allsoe theare be mainteigned, wt parte of the premises, and kept in good reparaciouns, two greate stone bridges, and divers ffoule and daungerous high wayes; the charge whereof the towne of hitsellfe ys not hable to mainteign; so that the Lacke thereof wilbe a greate noysaunce to the kinges maties subjectes passing to and ffrom the marches of wales, and an utter Ruyne to the same towne, - being one of the fairest and moste proffittuble townes to the kinges highnesse in all the Shyre* [8].

The seal of the Guild of the Holy Cross. With the decline of the deBirmingham family the Guild became an alternative government, laying out land for development, maintaining roads and bridges.

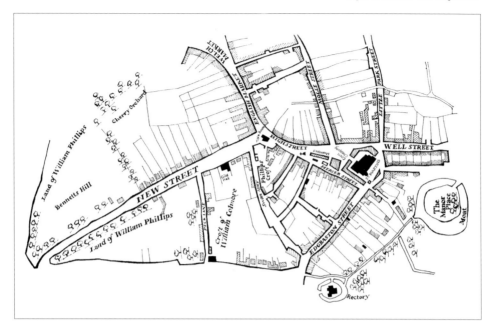

The Tudor town, based on Bickley and Hill's Plan of Birmingham, 1553.

Regrettably, at the suppression of the Guild, all its records, reports and accounts were confiscated by the King's Commissioners, and with them was lost the history of the town for a century and a half. What records we have are compiled from other sources, and, though incomplete, indicate that this alternative government of the town, conducted from the Guild Hall in New Street, was actively involved in the physical growth of Birmingham, in the form of street construction and house building. Rent from their properties was re-invested in the town. Some tenants of the Guild, who performed useful functions within the town, such as the common midwife and the town crier, lived rent-free. Sometime before 1437, the lord of the manor, William Bermyngeham, sold off part of Little Park, and a new street, Park Street (sometimes known as Little Park Street) came into being. Who actually developed it is not known, but by 1437 the Guild was renting out houses and land here. One John Crowe leased a messuage and a croft from the Guild at an annual rent of 7s and 4d [9]. Park Street was not in the original gift to the Guild, so evidently they were also buying up land and apparently developing it. At the break up of the Guild in 1553, self-interest, in the form of Commissioner, Thomas Holte, descendant of John atte Holte, came into play, and the good works of the Guild ceased. Holte and his brother-in-law succeeded in bringing much of the Guild's land into their own estates.

North of Birmingham an area later to become Sutton Coldfield fell under the benevolence of Bishop Vesey. He was born about 1462, the son of William Harman of Moor Hall. The bishop changed his name soon after 1507 and, after progressing through the Church, was appointed Bishop of Exeter in 1519. He was also President

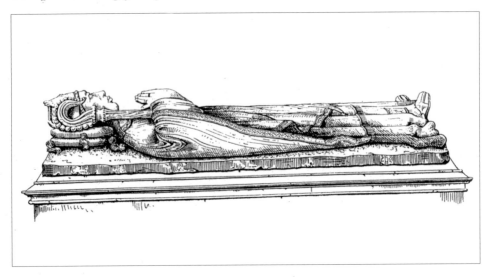

Effigy of Bishop Vesey in Holy Trinity church, Sutton Coldfield. Vesey built fifty stone houses for the people of Sutton.

of the Court of the Marches of Wales and at one time tutor to the Princess Mary. His many preferments made him a very rich man. He was by nature a generous man and when he returned to live in Sutton, did his utmost to improve the town. John Harman, alias Vesey, established a weekly market and an annual fair. He redeveloped the old market place, and founded a grammar school and endowed it. He enlarged the parish church by the addition of a new nave and chancel, and built a Town Hall with a prison beneath it. Vesey also arranged the building of two bridges over the river Tame at Curdworth and Water Orton. He also paid for the building of fifty-one stone houses for the populace, and established a cloth trade at Sutton. Of the houses built, twenty-one have been identified, of which eight have now been demolished. Other houses in the borough may survive, but have been greatly altered over the years. Several are clearly recognisable by their external stone-built chimneys and internal spiral staircases. The best examples are: Old Farm, Moor Hall Drive, Vesey Cottage near new Hall Mill, Wylde Green Road, The Old Stone House next to St Peter's church, Maney Hill Road, Warren House Farm off Walmley Road, High Heath Cottage off Withy Hill Road.

By the mid-sixteenth century Birmingham had progressed from a village to a small industrial town and had become a place of manufactured metal goods. John Leland in his *Itinerary of Britain* relates that he passed through Birmingham in 1538. He describes the town in the following manner:

I came through a pretty street or ever I entred into Bermingham towne. This street, as I remember, is called Dirtey. In it dwell smithes and cutlers, and there is a brooke that divideth this street from Bermingham, and is an Hamlett or Member belonging to the parish thereby.

Two of the stone houses Vesey had built.

> *There is at the end of Dirtey a proper chappell, and a mansion house of tymber hard on the*
> *ripe, as the brooke runneth downe; and as I went through the ford, by the bridge, the water ran*
> *downe on the right hand, and a few miles below goeth into Tame, ripa dextra. This brooke,*
> *above Dirtey, breaketh in two armes, that a little beneath the bridge close again. This brooke*
> *riseth, as some say, four or five miles above Bermingham, towards Black Hilles.*
>
> *The beauty of Bermingham, a good market towne in the extreame parts of Warwickshire, is*
> *one street going up alonge, almost from the left ripe of the brooke, up a meane hill, by the length*
> *of a quarter of a mile. I saw but one Parrock Church in the towne. There be many smiths in*
> *the towne that use to make knives and all mannour of cutting tooles, and many loriners that*
> *make bittes, and a great many naylors. Soe that a great part of the towne is maintained by*
> *smithes, who have their iron and sea-cole out of Staffordshire* [10].

'Dirtey' is, of course, Deritend. The 'brooke' is the river Rea. The 'proper chappell' was St John's, now demolished, and the 'mansion house of tymber' is the Old Crown. The 'ripe' is the bank of the river, and the 'one streete' is the High Street, which ran up past the 'Parrock' or parish church of St Martin.

A more detailed description of sixteenth-century Birmingham is revealed in the Survey of Birmingham, conducted by the King's Commissioners in 1553. All the freeholders of the town, some eighty-six in number, are named, as are its streets:

High Street	– the present extended Bull Ring, reaching up to the junction with New Street.
Corn Cheaping	– or corn market, the Bull Ring area.
Mercer Street, alias	
Spycers Street or Spiceal Street	– the western side of the Bull Ring.
English Market	– the present High Street from New Street.
Welch Market	– beginning halfway along the High Street and extending to Dale End, and also known as New Market Street.
Dale End	– the present street, and beyond it, Dale End Barrs.
Chappell Street	– the present Bull Street.
Priors Conyngre Lane	– Steelhouse Lane from Bull Street to Loveday Street.
New Street	– then only partially built up.
Ashford's Fordrove or Swan Alley	– taking its name from the Swan Inn at the junction of High Street and New Street.
Lea's Lane	– now disappeared underneath New Street Station.
Godd's Cart Lane	– now Carrs Lane.
Molle Street	– Moor Street.
Little Park Street	– Park Street, off the Bull Ring.
Well Street	– the top end of the present Digbeth High Street.

Malt Mill Lane	– Mill Lane, off Digbeth High Street.
Dygbeth	– Digbeth High Street.
Cawsey	– the High Street near the river Rea.
Deretend	– Deritend.
Bordesley	– High Street, Bordesley.

The survey refers to the richly endowed Priory and Free Chapel of St Thomas, surrounded by its extensive grounds. The Guild of the Holy Cross, and that of St John the Baptist in Deritend with its Free School, appear, as does the parish church of St Martin, with its endowed chantries. Old buildings now long gone, such as the Tolbooth or Town Hall, are mentioned. This two-storey building, at the junction of High Street and New Street, later became the Leather Hall, being used by the Leather Sealers to inspect the quality of leather put on sale in the town. It was from here, on the upper floor in a room about 50 feet long, that the Court Leet, the official government of the town, administered Birmingham. The ground floor was divided into several rooms, one of which was used as a prison until the new prison in Peck Lane was opened in 1697. Behind the Toll Booth was a large open space. Here was situated an ancient public well; by 1735 it was known as the 'draw-well'. Nearby was the Shambles, or Butchers' Row. These were a double row of half-timbered shops, all open to the street. Small in size, they were one and a half storeys in height. Separated from the High Street at their narrowest by just 9 yards, the Shambles were originally shop stalls belonging to the burgage tenements in the High Street. Originally they would have been dismantled at the end of each day's trading, but gradually they became fixed structures. Above the Shambles was the High Cross, also known as the Butter Cross and Market Cross, and latterly (after 1706) the Old Cross, to distinguish it from the New, or Welch Cross. Joseph Hill, the Victorian historian, refers to a deed of 1494, wherein the High Cross is mentioned, though undoubtedly it would have been much older. The Schedules of Tenancies of the Guild of the Holy Cross record, in 1547, that Thomas Cowper's house, the 'Mayden Hede', was situated here at the High Cross.

That part of the High Street, between New Street to a little way past Carrs Lane, was known as English Market, Rother Market or the Beast Market. 'Rother' is the Old English word for horned beasts. There is a Rother Street in Stratford-upon-Avon. It is probable that a beast market was held here in Birmingham every Thursday for several hundred years. Welch End, or Welch Market, was the continuation of the High Street. It was situated between Carrs Lane and Dale End. The market was so-called because it was here that the Welsh drovers established themselves around the old cross that was renamed after them. The earliest record of the cross being so named appears in a deed of 1642. In his will of that year, Robert Shelton refers to his property as a 'tenement scittuate in Birmingham neare the Welch Crosse now in the tenure of John Barney'. The Welsh had established themselves here by 1547, for in that year another deed records a property 'situate lying and being within the Borough of Birmingham county of Warwick aforesaid in the Welch End...'.

Some thirty-three years after, in 1586, William Camden's *Britannia* was published. The antiquary gives us some account of how the town had expanded and changed since the Survey of 1553. Camden relates that leaving Kenilworth:

> *I came next to Solyhill which has nothing remarkable but its church; then to Bromicham, swarming with inhabitants and echoing with the noise of anvils (for here are a great many smiths). The lower part of the town is very watery. The upper part rises with abundance of handsome buildings, and it is none of the least honours of the place that from hence the noble and warlike family of Bremichams in Ireland had their original and name.*

During the Civil War Birmingham supplied arms to Parliament's cause. As a result of the anti-Royalist stance of the townspeople, Birmingham was assaulted and pillaged by a Royalist army under the command of Prince Rupert. Over eighty houses were burnt down in the process, including much of Bull Street. At the end of the war the town's production of metalware continued at its wartime levels. London's plague and fire of 1665-66 was a golden opportunity for Birmingham's metal workers. With its industry crippled, the capital looked to Birmingham to supply the saws that cut wood, the chisels that made joints, the nails that held floorboards, joists and eaves, the hinges for doors and windows, the catches and locks that secured, and a myriad of other essential metal objects taken for granted in times of plenty. Birmingham men were not slow to respond. The brothers Humphrey and John Jennens organised the expansion of their iron trade with the capital. Thomas Pemberton, the Quaker ironmaster, 'hath orders in London so he sayeth £146 and £60…' (The Bustleholme Account Book records [12].)

When he died in 1671, Birmingham ironmonger John Milner had at his London warehouse 'A stock of nayles' valued at £116 9s 5d [13]. Milner was typical of the new breed of industrial entrepreneurs – wholesale dealers in ironware. These men purchased and distributed iron and other metals to smiths and metalworkers, then bought and sold their manufactured goods. Their markets were not only national, but also international. As early as 1623, in a list of goods carried into Ireland, there were Birmingham knives valued at one shilling and sixpence for ten [14]. Ligon, in his *History of Barbados* published in 1657, records that, 'Nailes of all sorts, with hooks, hinges, and cramps of iron … are to be had at Birmingham in Staffordshire [*sic*], much cheaper than in London'. What he was possibly unaware of was that the London goods were in all probability manufactured in Birmingham and purchased by London merchants for resale. One observer remarked in 1650 that 'all or most of the London ironmongers buy all or most of their nails and petty ironwork either from Birmingham, almost a hundred miles from London, or at London as brought from thence … all England … supplied from a single market [15]. Foreigners were not slow to appreciate Birmingham-manufactured goods either. Francois Maximilien Misson, while touring Italy, observed in Milan, 'Fine works of Rock Crystal, Swords, Heads for Canes, Snuff Boxes, and other fine works of steel', adding that they 'can be had better and cheaper at Birmingham' [16]. Birmingham had become a boomtown.

During the late seventeenth century, as the wealthier classes began moving out of the built-up town centre to new brick-built houses on the outskirts, their former large merchant houses, occupying medieval sites, were acquired by speculative builders. Invariably these houses had extensive gardens, and many had courtyards too. All this space became increasingly valuable as Birmingham's population grew. Examples of both infilling and the conversion of houses into tenements from the 1660s are well documented. In 1674 George Guest bought an area as small as 2 yards and 4 inches, facing onto Edgbaston Street for £2 and 10s. Along with the purchase went the right to 'join any building he may erect to the wall of the house' of his neighbour, Thomas Green [17].

Evidence for such activities in the 1680s suggests that a population explosion was occurring in Birmingham. This is confirmed by the baptismal register of St Martin's, which shows a rise in baptisms from seventy in 1680, to 210 in 1685. The town was bursting at the seams, and land was at a premium. The Roundabout House near St Martin's church, formerly in the possession of Barnaby Smith, was converted into four tenements. Nearby in Smith's former yard was a 'tenement newly erected upon part of the yard and in which John Vaughan dwells'. Across the yard, the Talbot Inn in Spicer Street was also divided into tenements, with 'four messuages built in the back part of the above mentioned messuage'. Just around the corner in Edgbaston Street, on a small plot, John Ruston built 'a shop, a room behind the shop, a chamber over the shop, a room over the entry next to the shop and a tenement standing behind the said shop and room containing a lower room, an upper room and a garratt and also the Beame house hovel, lyme pitts, water pitts and two gardens thereto belonging' [18].

Added to this piecemeal development was the construction of new streets. The first of these new streets was Phillip Street. It was named after the owner of the land, Robert Phillips. Though of an ancient Birmingham family, he was then a resident of Newton Regis. Phillips had leased out his land fronting onto the High Street to Shem Bracebridge, a London haberdasher. Bracebridge, with a long-term tenure, built four houses on land between Rotton's garden and the Swan Inn. These were to be some of the last timber-framed houses built in Birmingham. In 1692, Richard Pinley, a bricklayer, leased land along the new street from Phillips for a term of ninety-nine years at a yearly rent of 13s and 4d. On this land he built two houses. Phillips leased further land to William Inge, who subleased it to John Blun, a joiner, for a term of eighty-six years. Blun covenanted 'to build within the space of three years, a new house according to the mode and fashion of the rest of the houses in Phillips Street' [19]. Six months later Pinley subleased further land to Thomas Newcomb, on the same proviso.

Pinley and Robert Bridgens, a carpenter, in association with builder Joseph Hands, were responsible for the development of nearby Colmore Street. On 1 August 1690 they leased School Croft from William Colmore for a term of ninety-nine years at an annual rental of £15. The indenture records their intention to 'build several new houses and to make a street through the said croft 9 yards broad leading from Peck

Lane towards the new buildings of Robert Phillips Esq., called Phillips Street' [20]. The street was developed by 1692 and contained not only houses but also shops.

Like Phillips and Colmore, William Bell, then resident at Alvechurch, now decided to develop his property between Worcester Street and High Street. An agreement was drawn up between Bell and the developers: Richard Danckes a brickmaker, Thomas Kempsey a timberman, John Blun a joiner and John Beate. Bell laid down building regulations in a seven-clause agreement. His stated intention was that the street, which was to be named after him, 'and the buildings thereof on both sides', shall 'be uniforme handsome and comodius and therefore the more gracefull and pleasant to such persons as shall inhabit therein' [21]. The builders agreed to complete the houses within three years, and construct a street, pitched with good stones.

There then followed the development of existing streets, and in particular Edgbaston Street and Smallbrook Street. Thomas Fewster leased land from which he was permitted to extract clay for bricks and tiles, provided that he built houses on attached land. This he did, selling the houses for £60 each, with a ground rent of sixteen shillings and sixpence a year. The permission to take clay for bricks reflects the change in house construction in Birmingham from timber framed to brick. The buildings erected in Phillips, Bell and Colmore Streets were designed to house the skilled artisans of the town. For those who had risen to the estate of gentleman, more substantial houses were required. There were two such developments, Temple Row, and the first planned estate constructed on the site of the old priory and park.

two

The First Planned Estate

The lands of the Priory of St Thomas the Apostle came into the possession of the Holte family following the priory's suppression in 1547. They sold the estate to the Smallbrooke family, and in 1697 John Pemberton, a Quaker ironmonger, purchased part of the estate. Sometime later he purchased the remainder. Upon completing his purchase, Pemberton laid out the estate for development. The designer is generally supposed to have been architect and carpenter William Westley. He provided convenient, though narrow, streets with a square as the focal point of the new development. Like other landowners, Pemberton conveyed plots to developers. The names are familiar, and include Thomas Kempsey, Thomas Lane and Richard Pinley. Prices of plots varied from £2 a yard for land fronting Bull Street, to £1 in the Square and adjoining streets. The back land went for 1s a yard. Before any land was conveyed to a purchaser, Pemberton had to erect and finish his building. Money towards the cost of building was invariably borrowed. With the Priory Estate, Pemberton's brother-in-law, Sampson Lloyd, was generally the lender.

Thomas Kempsey built the sixteen houses in the Square, which were completed by 1707. Purchasers agreed not to use their premises for butchers, bakers or blacksmiths shops. Nor were they permitted to erect any muck hill or dung hill, or to keep pigs. The first known occupiers were:

South-west angle
  John Pemberton (ironmonger)
  John Pemberton (gentleman)
  Samuel Swynfen (doctor)
  Daniel Whalley (ironmonger)

South-east angle
  Mrs Wall
  Mr Samuel Stewart
  William Acock jr (gentleman)
  Richard Baddily

North-east angle
  John Wilkes
  Henry Bradford
  Mrs Beal
  Joseph Farmer (ironmonger)

North-west angle
  John Fidoe (ironmaster)
  Mr Eborall (gentleman)
  James Billingsley (gentleman)
  Randle Bradburn (ironmonger)

The residents were a mixture of gentry and successful industrialists. Their houses were originally leasehold for a term of 1,000 years, with a known purchase price in one instance of £100 [1].

Richard Pinley, Stephen Newton and Thomas Lane developed the Upper Minories and Upper Priory at the same time. In January 1707 Newton and Pinley purchased 19 yards of Upper Priory, 'designed for a street leading from the Square into Whitehalls Lane…' [2]. In February, Lane purchased 15 yards and the Newton-Pinley partnership acquired a further 14 yards. They all agreed to erect houses or other buildings upon the land facing the street, 'the buildings to be as high and regular as those now built' [3]. Again there were restrictions forbidding the letting of buildings to 'a butcher – who shall keep a slaughter house or a smith who would keep a smithy'.

Newton Street, named after Thomas Newton, was the next street developed on the estate. The new road was 10 yards wide. Plots were measured out with frontages of 10 yards, 2 feet and 6 inches, and lay to a depth of 40 yards. Houses followed the customary three storeys in height. Begun in 1708, the last houses were completed by 1710, and sold for £100. Newton was also responsible for the laying out of Lichfield Street between the Square and Newton Street. Lane, who also built along St John Street and St Thomas Street, did further building. Westley's Row was developed quite late. Surviving deeds date from 1722. The Row was named after William Westley, a carpenter who, as we saw earlier, is generally credited with designing the Priory Estate. He also drew the first known map of Birmingham in 1731 and two prospects, one depicts an eastern view of the town, drawn from the top of Cooper's windmill, the second is of the newly built St Philip's church and Temple Row.

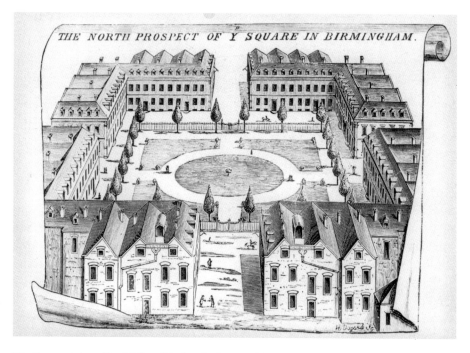

The Square, designed by William Westley, focal point of the Priory Estate.

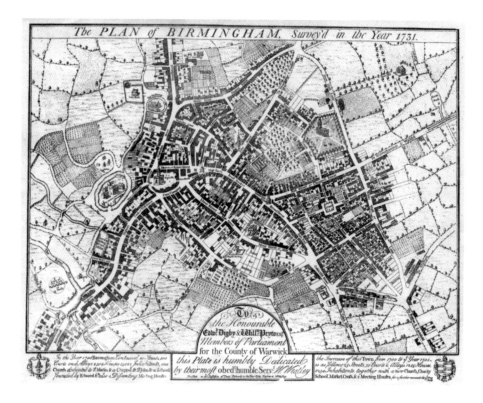

William Westley's Plan of Birmingham, 1731.

In many ways St Philip's, with its High Town parish, marked the new Birmingham, as opposed to the old medieval town. The site for the church consisted of 4 acres of land on the brow of the hill, overlooking the old town. Known by the name of Horse Close, it was owned by Elizabeth, widow of Robert Phillips. The Church Commissioners first met at the Swan Inn on 23 May 1709, and resolved 'to go on with all expedition and lay the foundation stone this summer' [4]. Thomas Archer of Umberslade designed the church in the Baroque style. In August the stone was laid and the commissioners agreed 'to contract with workmen, to lay materials'. Some of the names are familiar. The bricklayers who built the new church were John Cash, Richard Pinley and John Willinger. With Thomas Lane, Willinger had also built the 'Old Cross' in 1705. Later, in partnership, Willinger, Pinley and Cash worked on the building of King Edward's 'Great School' in the late 1720s and early 1730s. The stonemason at St Philip's was Joseph Pedley, and the carpenters were William Westley, Thomas Lane and Thomas Ruston.

Symbolic of the new town, St Philip's was built of brick and faced in stone. The brickmaker is unknown, but the probable source of material was Brick Kiln Close, situated at the junction of the present Broad Street and Easy Row. William Hill in the commissioners' book duly entered the bricklayers' contract:

> *We do promise and agree with the said Commissioners that having bricks delivered in the Horse Close at 8s per thousand and sand gotten and water allowed, we will well and substantially lay ye said brick and find lime and all other materials belonging to a bricklayer, and build ye said church according to ye draught now agreed on by £3 per rod; and that we have a hundred of boards to make mortar tubes, and that ye work is begun to go on with all convenient speed we can.*
>
> *7th of March 1710*

There was a well at Horse Close which would have provided bricklayers with water. This was needed not only for mixing the tubs of mortar, alluded to in the contract, but also for keeping the walls moist. Joseph Moxen in his *Mechanick Excercises or the Doctrine of Handworks,* published in 1703, advised, 'If you lay your bricks in the Summer … throw Pales of Water onto the Wall after the bricks are lay'd … which will make the wall much stronger'. With the brick walls complete, Joseph Pedley now began facing the brickwork, according to his contract of 9 March 1710:

> *I, Joseph Pedley do promise and agree to do ye plain of ye Stone Work for 2½d per foot, and ye Moldings at 7d per foot; but if the Commissioners do find that 7d per foot, for the said Moldings, be not enough, they do give something more.*

Pedley ordered his stone from William Shakespeare's Rowington Quarry. 'Two hundred loads of stone at four shillings a load; each load containing twenty-feet broken according to ye scantlings [specifications] … was bought'. Other stone came from Umberslade.

Houses in Temple Row, designed by William Westley.

The carpenters continued the work. The original flooring of St Philip's was of wood. William Westley and the other carpenters then undertook 'to put up the furrings [planks] of the gallery for five shillings and sixpence per square, and to find all the scaffolding for the whole of the church for five and thirty pounds'. They also agreed 'to do all the framework of the roof for ten shillings and sixpence per square'. The joiners now completed the more delicate and intricate woodwork, most of which was completed in oak. The plasterers took over, and finally Richard Huss agreed to whitewash the whole of the work. St Philip's was consecrated on 5 October 1715. Shortly afterwards a row of houses known as Temple Row was built overlooking the churchyard. This row consisted of ten houses divided into two blocks by Cherry Street. The builders are unknown, but in view of the continuing partnership of Willinger, Pinley and Cash, these men are the likely contenders. The architect too is unknown, but an obvious candidate would be William Westley. He drew *The North Prospect of St Philip's Church &c. in Birmingham,* printed and published in 1732. The row is seen clearly in the background, and the Square, appears as an inset. The whole appears to be an early form of advertising, declaring Westley's talents as a builder. A portrait of Westley, now in the Birmingham Museum and Art Gallery, shows him holding a plan of St Philip's.

The houses in Temple Row were of brick, with moulded stone string–courses over the ground and first-floor windows. The windows had stone radiated-lintels with projecting keystones, and the entrances, with the known exception of what was to become No. 37, had plain moulded doorheads, over which were small windows to light the halls. No. 37 had an ogee broken pediment above its entrance.

There is a brief reference to Temple Row, or Tory Row as it was sometimes mockingly called because of its inhabitants, in William Toldervey's *England and Wales Described in a Series of Letters,* published in 1762. In Letter XXXVI, Toldervey relates that as he entered Birmingham from the western side, the first notable building that he saw was St Philip's church. This he described as standing,

> *in the Middle of a large Church-yard, around which is a beautiful walk, adorned with trees like those in Lincoln's Inn Gardens. On one side of this Church-yard the Buildings are as lofty, elegant, and uniform as those of Bedford-Row, and inhabited by People of Fortune, who are great wholesale Dealers in the Manufacture of this Town… These Buildings have the appellation of Tory Row; and this is the highest and genteelest Part of the Town of Birmingham.*

In half a lifetime Birmingham had changed dramatically from a town of half-timbered houses to one of brick. The period 1680 to 1720 was a watershed. It saw a change from craft, as represented by wood, to industry, as represented by brick. So grand was the scale of change, that not only where there new developments, but the old town too was transformed. Buildings of brick came to symbolise the new industrial town of Birmingham.

three

The Georgian Town

I first saw Birmingham July 14, 1741, and will therefore perambulate its boundaries at that time with my traveller, beginning at the top of Snow-hill, keeping the town on our left, and the fields that then were, on our right.

Through Bull-lane we proceed to Temple-street; down Peck Lane, to the top of Pinfold-street; Dudley-street, the Old Hinkleys to the top of Smallbrook-street, back through Edgbaston-street, Digbeth, to the upper end of Deritend. We shall return through Park-street, Masshouse-lane, the North of Dale end, Stafford-street, Steelhouse-lane, to the top of Snow-hill, from whence we set out.

From 1741, to the present year 1780, Birmingham, seems to have acquired the amazing augmentation of seventy one streets, 4172 houses, and 25,032 inhabitants.

William Hutton, *An History of Birmingham, 1780.*

How this great change came about is the subject of this chapter. The estates of the Colmore, Phillips and Inge families, covering much of the sandstone ridge to the north of the existing town, lying between Easy Row and Snow Hill, had not as yet become available for building. The Phillips' land, comprising two closes, Bennett's Hill and Banner Close, lying between St Philip's church and the top of New Street, were tied up as agricultural land in 1698 for a term of 120 years. On the southern edge of the town was the old manorial land of Colborne Fields, then in the tenure of Dr Sherlock, who would not permit it to be developed. William Hutton wrote that Sherlock believed 'his land was valuable, and if built upon, his successor, at the expiration of the term would have the rubbish to carry off'. In his will Sherlock prohibited his successors from granting building leases [1]. At Five Ways there was a further large parcel of undeveloped Glebe land belonging to St Martin's.

By and large the Priory Estate satisfied the needs of the expanding town at the time. The Weaman Estate, on the north-eastern edge of the town, which was also developed from the early eighteenth century, further eased the pressure. Coupled to this were a number of small speculative schemes dating from the mid–eighteenth century. In October 1733 William Hay, a toymaker, leased part of Guest's Cherry Orchard from Moses Guest. He also laid out Cannon Street, 10 yards broad, as a means of access to it from New Street. Hay developed the site, and constructed a second road linking up Guest's with the nearby Walker's Cherry Orchard, so that it too could be developed. The road was appropriately called Cherry Street. In 1742 Joseph Rann, a butcher, bought further land here and developed the site. Other streets and squares came into existence. In November 1743, John Hands built the square named after him. Within the square he built eight tenements. In March 1766 Benjamin Brettell leased part of a close situated between Snow Hill and Groom Street, also known as Livery Street. Across it he cut a street 5 yards and 1 foot wide, which he named after himself. His building plots were 6 yards wide, falling back to a depth of 70 yards. In 1775 William Mansell developed Price Street, on the edge of the Weaman Estate. His plots were 11½ yards onto the street, with a depth of 46 feet. Down by the river Rea, Edward Hastin, a builder, leased Porter's Meadow from Charles Glover for 117 years. Across it he cut Rea Street in April 1786, promising to build one or more dwelling houses fronting onto it within the year.

The expansion of industry was the key to growth. Building resumed on a grand scale in 1746, when prominent local families, many of whom had moved away from Birmingham, now made their land available for building use. First was the Colmore family, then the Jennens, and finally the Gooch, Inge and Legge families. There was also infilling on smaller estates lying in between, such as the Prinsep family, Lench's Trust, the Free School and the development at Ashted, to the east of the town. All this building prompted *Aris's Gazette* to comment in 1759, '…there are now more new buildings carrying on in this town than have been for many years past and more contracted for, that only want for hands to execute, which at this time are very much wanted'.

The Weaman Estate

Land on the Weaman Estate was released for building in the early eighteenth century. Westley's Plan of Birmingham for 1731 shows that both Weaman Street and Slaney Street had been laid out, and Kettle's Steel Houses, which were to give their name to Steelhouse Lane, were in existence. In 1735 William Phillips leased land from Anna Slaney on the edge of the estate, and built houses. Development on the estate itself, though, was slow. By 1750 Sand Street, leading off from Weaman Street towards the yet as un-named Catherine Street, had been cut and named, though no houses had been built. To renew interest in the development, sisters Dorothy and Mary Weaman obtained a private Act of Parliament in 1772 to erect a chapel of ease to St Martin's. The cost of building was raised by subscription, and Mary Weaman contributed £1,200. The church was dedicated to St Mary. The Lench's Trust agreed to an

St Mary's church, focal point of the Weaman Estate.

exchange of adjoining land so that a new street across their land could be cut, they 'being desirous to assist in promoting so pious a design and apprehending that the building of a church upon the land of the said Dorothy Weaman and Mary Weaman will increase the value of such of their lands as lye adjacent to the said intended church…'[2] The church in the newly cut Whittall Street, designed by Joseph Pickford in the Classical style, was an octagonal brick building with a small tower and spire, standing in a large churchyard.

The sisters had formerly sold land for building, but after the construction of the church in 1774, they began making leases as the land increased in value. On 1 May 1782, the sisters issued a lease of 111 years on a piece of land measuring 6 yards onto the intended extension of Loveday Street, to a depth of 38 yards, to Richard Newman, a button maker. He covenanted to build within the space of one year one or more dwelling houses, at a minimum expenditure of £100. That same day they issued two more leases, under the same conditions, to John Berry, a jeweller and William Hadley, a bone-mould turner. Hadley's land adjoined the land of an existing lessee, Henry Crumpton [3].

The gun industry in Birmingham was in its early days spread out within the town, with a concentration of workshops requiring water, notably the barrel makers, situated in Digbeth. The increasingly complex division of labour between workshops, and the importance of rapid communication between them, saw the migration of the trade to the Weaman Estate from 1777. The houses, which began life as the residences of wealthier arms manufacturers, with workshops in the rear, were eventually given over to the use of workmen, so that within twenty years the estate had become known as the 'Gun Quarter'. G.C. Allen in his *Industrial Development of Birmingham and the Black Country*, gives details of a workshop in the quarter in the following century:

Anderton's Square on the Weaman Estate. The estate later became the 'Gun Quarter' of the city.

Thomas Hanson's Plan of Birmingham, 1781. Note the Colmore Estate based on St Paul's church. The canals to the south ensured industrial expansion and further development.

A passage from a main street communicates with a court-yard, from which two blocks of two-storied buildings rise, facing one another; and at intervals staircases lead up from the courtyard to the workshops, of which the buildings are entirely composed. Each shop consists of one or two small rooms, in which the various operations in connection with the setting-up of guns are performed. In one shop, two men will be found engaged in barrel-browning; in another a single workman is shaping the gun-stocks from a pile of roughly cut wooden blocks, delivered to him by the master gunmaker. Elsewhere a lock filer is working with one assistant and in another shop, leading from the same staircase, an engraver and his sons carry on their trade. Farther down the street, a narrow alley communicates with an ill-lighted room, where two barrel filers, whose work is known throughout Europe, are engaged; and nearby in a tiny workshop, with the name of the proprietor chalked on the door, which forms the establishment of one of the most famous hardeners in the trade. Each craftsman works for one or several gunmakers, and receives the material from them; but hires his own workshop and pays his own assistants.

The Colmore Estate

The Colmore family arrived in Birmingham in the mid-fifteenth century. By trade they were cloth merchants. They rose to prominence, and both William Colmore and his son, William jr, were original governors of the Free School. In 1619 the family entered its pedigree and arms at the time of the Visitation of Warwickshire.

The Colmores had their family home in the High Street, but in the early seventeenth century moved to the estate of New Hall, on the northern edge of the town, upon which the family mansion stood for nearly 200 years. By 1746 the family had long left Birmingham and were established in Middlesex.

The 100-acre Colmore Estate to the north of the town became available under a private Act of 1746, granting building leases of 120 years. Three smaller parcels of land, comprising some further 50 acres to the west and south-east of the town, also became available. The first sites were leased in 1747. By 1750 most of Colmore Row and Ann Street had been fully developed. By the 1770s the estate had been developed as far as Lionel Street, and the rest of the land had been surveyed for building, with several streets 20 yards wide, as is witnessed on Hanson's Plan of Birmingham for 1778. In addition Charles Colmore also provided 3 acres for a church and graveyard, donating £1,000 towards its construction. Around this square, with its much higher rents, were built the finest houses on the estate. The Colmore Estate leased plots from 200 to 3,000 square yards. These were intended for houses with a frontage onto the road of 5, 20 or 30 yards. In 1764 the estate was charging 1½d per square yard, rising to 2d by 1785. The larger plots were intended to provide room for tenements and workshops in the rear. Samuel Avery, a bricklayer, acquired one of the first lots leased along Colmore Row in 1747. On his 20 x 50-yard plot he erected four houses on half of the land, the remainder he conveyed to a carpenter and joiner. Indeed the majority of builders along Colmore Row between 1747 and 1750 were craftsmen related to the building trade. Little attempt was made in the early days to control the nature of construction other than that the building should have a minimum amount spent on its construction (e.g. £120 in 1750, £140 in 1753); that it should be three storeys high, and have cellarage, and follow the building line along the street. A typical house along Great Charles Street, sold in June 1822, gives details of one such construction. It possessed on its top storey five lodging rooms, three dressing rooms, a closet and water closet. On the middle storey were two lodging rooms, two dressing rooms, two closets and a drawing room measuring 22 feet by 15½ feet. On the ground floor was a front parlour 17 feet by 15½ feet, a dining parlour 22 feet by 16½ feet, a china closet, store room and butler's pantry. In the lower apartments, below ground, was a breakfast parlour 17 feet by 15½ feet, a kitchen 22 feet by 16½ feet, a pantry and good larder, with cellarage under the whole. Behind the house was a flagged court with a brew house, pantry pump and other outhouses.

New Hall, the Colmore family home, was eventually pulled down in 1787. It had been leased to the great industrialist Matthew Boulton and used by him as a warehouse. The house had stood near the junction of Newhall Street and Great Charles Street. With its demolition, building resumed, and by the early nineteenth century the whole estate was built upon.

The Jennens Estate

William Jennens, who settled in Birmingham in the middle of the sixteenth century, founded the Jennens dynasty. Upon his death in 1602, his accumulated wealth was left to his two sons, John and Ambrose. They were dealers in iron, and by 1700 John's son, Humphrey, was one of the biggest landowners in Warwickshire. By the eighteenth century the family provided the country with two millionaires, one of whom, dying intestate, brought the family national fame as the 'Jarndyce' family in Dickens's *Bleak House*. The family moved from their High Street mansion to Erdington Hall, and had their land in Birmingham laid out for building. In an indenture dated 29 November 1729, Thomas Terrawest was granted a piece of land fronting Chappell Street, 9 yards in width, onto the street. For this he paid £27. The next month Hannah Walthew, a widow, purchased land along the same road for £15. Development seems to have been slow, possibly because the area was perceived to be isolated, and on the edge of the town. As an incentive to development, the church of St Bartholomew was built in 1749 as a chapel of ease to St Martin's. John Jennens donated the site of the church and his wife gave £1,000 towards its construction.

Above left: The Act of Parliament for development of the Colmore Estate.

Above right: A sales catalogue detailing a typical house on the Colmore Estate's main arterial road, Great Charles Street.

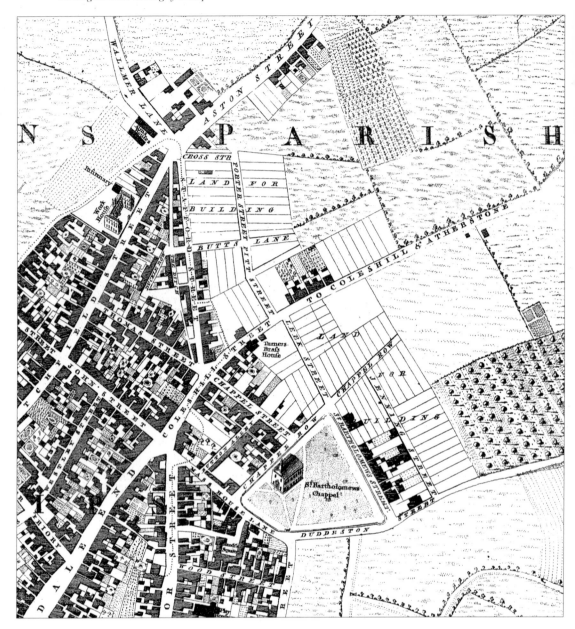

The Jennens Estate, laid out for building. Detail from Samuel Bradford's Plan of Birmingham, 1750.

When St Bartholomew's was built, it stood on the eastern edge of the town, surrounded, as Samuel Bradford's Plan of 1750 shows, by 'Land for Building'. John Collins, a carpenter, leased several plots on the estate for a term of ninety-nine years in January 1749. Plots were smaller now, generally 5 yards onto the newly cut roads, and stretched back some 44 yards. Builders covenanted to build,

St Bartholomew's church, focal point of the Jennens Estate.

substantial dwelling house … three storeys high, the fronts of which houses shall not contain less
than one brick and a half in thickness from the foundation to the top of the second storey and
the back-parts not less than a brick and a half up to the first floor and not less than one brick
from thence to the tops thereof making use of the best bricks, timber and other materials and tile
the same with the best Yardley tiles and will Cornish the same with brick and stone cornishes
and set up palisades at the front or fronts and shall … expend the sum of £100 [4].

By 1810 the whole area had been developed, and the church sat in the middle of a
well-populated area.

The Inge Estate

This was a small estate of tiny pockets of land situated within Birmingham. It was
owned by a family then resident in Staffordshire. Their Birmingham estates were
tied up by marriage settlements, permitting short leases only, of twenty-one years
maximum. Private Acts of Parliament from 1753 to 1825 obtained longer leases,
thus enabling the family to benefit more profitably from their land. Perhaps the
most profitable development was that of Queen Street. Over the years, builder John
Lewis leased 3,448 square yards of land from the family. He made £2,900 on twenty
houses that he sold here in four lots between January 1777 and June 1786.

The Gooch Estate

The next substantial estate to be laid out for building was that of Sir Thomas Gooch. It was a diffuse estate divided principally into three large portions of land. It comprised land to the west of Pinfold Street and abutting on the north of what was to become Broad Street; land lying either side of Bromsgrove Street and south almost to the river Rea, and land to the east of Digbeth High Street, stretching down to the river and east towards Duddeston Street.

Sir Thomas of Benacre Hall, Suffolk, inherited the land from his uncle, Thomas Sherlock, Bishop of London. In a private Act passed in 1766, the reason given for development was 'the great want of houses' in Birmingham 'which hath of late years greatly increased in its trade and business, and number of inhabitants'. The Act permitted Gooch to consolidate his land by the exchange of plots, thus enabling him to make new streets without cutting across the land of his neighbours. According to tradition, his uncle, Bishop Sherlock, had refused to grant building leases, fearing that his land would become burdensome to his successors. Gooch had no such qualms. The estate was surveyed by John Snape and laid out in plots. The western block of land, comprising some 40 acres, was laid out in a grid pattern of 209 plots, with ten streets, including two main roads. Its attraction for manufacturers and merchants was the canal wharf situated here, which offered cheap transport. Between 1766 and 1780 Gooch leased 139 plots, and a further sixty-two in the decade that followed. Gooch was equally fortunate when the Warwick & Birmingham Canal Company proposed to cut their canal through

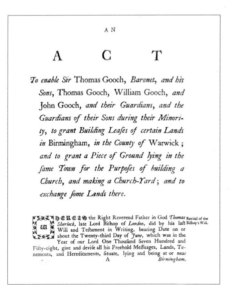

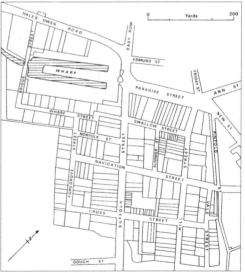

Above left: The Act of Parliament for development of the Gooch Estate.

Above right: The Gooch Estate laid out for development, based on Pye's plan. Note the canal wharf that led the industrial expansion and the growth of the town.

his Digbeth property. In an agreement of 29 July 1795, Gooch sold land to the company, which agreed to pay him a yearly rent of £149 10s 0d. Along the canal Gooch put out tenders for the construction of wharfs and warehouses. This part of the estate was eventually developed with a dozen or more streets from the mid-1780s. Leases were charged at an annual rate of 2d a square yard. A typical lease relating to property here is one given on 6 November 1788, being a lease for 109 years from Sir Thomas Gooch to William White of Birmingham, steel toy maker. Along a new street called Bordesley Street, on a plot 16 yards wide by 57 yards deep, White covenanted 'to erect two or more substantial dwelling houses'. In that same year on the more lucrative Gooch Estate site on the north-western part of the town, complete with its canal wharf, Sir Thomas leased a piece of ground at the junction of Summer Street and Navigation Street to John Woodstock for a term of 108 years. Woodstock agreed within the space of one year to 'erect four or more substantial dwelling houses to front Summer Street at a minimum expenditure of £450'.

Situated at the corner of Hurst Street and Inge Street, one block of houses in a courtyard survives as a last remaining portion of the original Gooch Estate development. They are back-to-back houses, typical of those being built in Birmingham from the end of the eighteenth century, and a model for some of the worst slum housing that was to be built in Birmingham in the early to mid-nineteenth century. Sir Thomas Gooch leased the site to builder John Wilmore in 1789. The houses were designed and built for occupation by artisan and labouring classes and are now to be restored and preserved as a museum.

During the 1770s the population increased from 30,804 in 1770 to 48,252 by 1778, leading to an increase in housing stock from 6,025 to 8,042. The opening of the Birmingham Canal, between Birmingham and the Black Country, with its terminus on the Gooch Estate, had halved the cost of importing coal into the town, encouraging the expansion of the metal trades. The production of metalware was an important stimulus to urban development. In addition, Birmingham also acted as the main service area for the West Midlands, providing merchant employers, suppliers of raw materials and the marketing of the finished product. The stimulation of the wartime demand for small arms during this time, boosted local trade and encouraged the continuation of building. According to Hutton, between 1778 and 1780 340 additional houses were built [6]. Building reached its peak between 1790 and 1792. Nearly all of the land on the Colmore Estate was built upon by this date. A new village, Islington, built on the land of the Rector of Birmingham, John Parsons, had come into being at Five Ways. It was created by a private Act of 1773, enabling the rector to parcel out plots of land for building on the 23-acre site, bounded by Broad Street, Islington Row and Bath Street. Leases were granted for up to 120 years.

An Account of the Number of the Houses, and Inhabitants Male and Female in the Town of Birmingham 1770

H. at the top of the Columns stand for Houses. M. for Males, and F. for Females, in each Street.

Street	H	M	F	Street	H	M	F
				Cherry Street	3	98	109
Anthony Street	52	123	136	Church Street	35	--	--
Aston Street	77	179	183	Coach Yard	14	22	35
Alcester Street Deritend	19	51	45	Colmore Row	35	83	111
Bath Street	6	16	11	Colmore Street	61	153	154
Barr's Square	9	25	40	Collins Court	13	41	30
Bell Street	31	88	84	Coleshill Street	134	351	331
Bow Street	81	203	190	Corbett's Alley	6	18	14
Bread Street	4	6	7	Cracknall's Yard	8	15	24
Brittles Yard	2	6	7	Cross Street	34	60	80
Brown's Court	21	53	44	Dale End	188	455	456
Brickiln Lane	44	113	109	Day's Buildings	6	9	9
Bordsley	100	231	266	Deritend	178	444	471
Boxing Alley	10	25	16	Digbeth	214	543	526
Buck Street	10	26	29	Doe Street	13	30	35
Bull Street	109	316	314	Dog Yard	5	15	14
Bull Lane	18	42	42	Dudley Street	82	257	250
Bull Ring	54	141	127	Edgbaston Street	149	409	382
Butts	79	170	188	Edmond Street	116	327	302
Cabbage Row	8	17	15	Exeter Row	23	39	50
Candlestick Alley	13	31	36	Floodgate Street	38	106	100
Cannon Street	45	90	106	Freeman Street	17	46	52
Carey's Court	22	41	46	Friday Street	21	47	59
Carr's Lane	50	91	116	Froggery	27	69	73
Castle Street	21	47	66	Gosty Green	44	111	107
Catherine Street	36	92	96	Great Charles Street	32	64	73
Chain Yard				Green-Tree Yard	5	19	11
& Potter's Ditto	8	19	30	Grosvenor Street	3	14	7
Chapel Row	76	143	136	Hand's Yard	12	24	31
Chapel Street	19	38	38	Hand's Square	26	49	62
Charles Street	80	211	188	Hicks's Square	6	15	15

Higgins's Yard	5	11	16	Priory Upper	24	67	51
High Street	200	545	542	Priory Lower	18	50	45
Hill Street	52	137	131	Queen Street	43	93	99
Hinkleys Old	52	154	131	Russel Street	9	25	22
Hinkleys New	59	151	174	Sand Street	12	30	30
Holloway Head	48	113	121	Slaney Street	79	268	206
Hollow-tooth Yard	9	25	27	Smallbrook Street			
Horse-shoe Yard	4	12	11	and Lady-well	111	296	284
Jenning Street	39	72	66	Snow Hill	135	415	406
John's Street	63	163	190	Spiceal Street	43	97	102
King Street	11	14	20	Square	18	34	38
Lamb Yard	5	14	19	St Martin's Lane	8	21	18
Lees Lane	41	89	95	Stafford Street	47	111	125
Lichfield Street	116	344	325	Steelhouse Lane	130	367	326
Little Lovely Street	8	18	21	Temple Street	47	116	138
Livery Street	50	128	122	Temple Street, Lowe	3	5	7
London 'Prentice Street	59	190	173	Temple Row	17	27	51
Lovely Street	22	61	58	Thomas's Street	64	164	157
Mass-house Lane	20	59	54	Topham's Row	14	30	32
Milk Street	16	31	36	Upper Minories	1	3	3
Mill Lane	12	28	32	Vale Street	33	75	73
Mill Lane, Lowe	49	92	112	Vauxhall Row	15	42	37
Moat Lane	54	141	120	Walmer Lane	74	165	157
Moore's Row	12	36	28	Weaman Street	164	507	443
Mount pleasant	47	166	130	Windmill Street	23	50	45
Navigation Row	14	25	33	Wood Street	40	121	111
Needless Alley	40	90	100	Worcester Street	76	216	190
New England	8	21	11	Alms House in	1	10	45
Newhall Street	48	113	126	Charity School	1	60	32
Newton Street	33	76	79	Dissenting School	1	17	9
Newmarket Street	5	9	8	Workhouse	1	161	201
New Meeting Street	18	32	54				
New Street	99	219	272				
Nova Scotia Street	38	105	86				
Old Meeting Street	50	140	166				
Over the Shamble	16	31	33				
Paradise Row	42	121	135				
Park Street	163	424	412				
Peck Lane	33	86	103				
Phillip Street	37	97	99				
Pinfold Street	114	233	269				
Potter Street	16	31	39				

6025 Houses, 15363 Males,
15441 Females

_____

30804 Total

Source: Sketchley's Directory of Birmingham.

Development continued east of the river Rea, along Bradford Street. As early as 1767 landowner Henry Bradford had sought to develop his property here. There was a certain reluctance to build here, as the lower end of the street named after him cut through the river's flood plain. In order to overcome this problem he initially offered land freehold to developers:

> *To be given gratis, some fee land pleasantly situated for building on, in Bradford Street, Deritend,*
> *to any person that will build upon the said land and carry on a considerable trade there.*
>
> Aris's Gazette, 3 August 1767

In 1771 Bradford was offering leasehold land up near Camp Hill at ¾d a square yard, as opposed to the north-western part of the Gooch Estate where it fetched 1½d a square yard. By 1778 Bradford Street was a well built-up street, surrounded by others such as Lombard and Moseley Streets, which were laid out, if not fully developed. A couple of the original buildings in Bradford Street still survive.

The Holte/Legge Estate

The Holt/Legge Estate occupied some 100 acres or more, on the north-east side of the town, around Gosta Green and north into Aston Parish. The Holte family had been the owners of Aston Hall, and latterly Erdington Hall. They had leased off small portions of land and in 1744 leased land in Woodcock Street to Isaac Stevens, a brick-maker, so that he could extract clay for making bricks and tiles. It was in 1788, after the estate had passed to Heneage Legge, son of the Earl of Dartmouth, that a private Act of Parliament (57 Geo. III, c.38), enabled the new owner to fully exploit his asset. In May 1788, Heneage Legge leased 3,476 square yards of land to John Powell of Birmingham, brick-maker. This large plot was situated at the junction of Woodcock Street and Holte Street. The land was let for a term of ninety-nine years at an annual rent of £30. The earmark of this and other such transactions was close attention to detail, going so far as to dictate detailed specifications regarding dimensions of houses, with stone cornices and stone sills to windows. By 1820 much of the estate had been built up, or at least its streets had been laid out.

The Ashted Estate

This development, situated to the east of the town, had formerly been the country estate of Dr John Ash, the prime mover in the establishment of the General Hospital. On 12 April 1771, Ash leased some 28 acres of land from Sir Charles Holte of Erdington Hall, for a term of ninety-nine years at a yearly rent of £80 [7]. Following Ash's departure from the town in 1787, John Brooke, an attorney, secured this estate and a further 41 acres, contiguous to Ash's estate, by an assignment in November of that year, from Sir Charles Holte, at a cost of £4,200. Brooke named the new estate Ashted, in honour of Dr Ash, and laid it out in building plots. At the centre of the new estate was Ash's mansion, now converted to a church and dedicated to St James. Brooke initially promoted the estate from the point of view of health, in that it was 'not likely to be surrounded by buildings … very inviting to ladies and gentlemen wanting a pleasing retirement'. Later however it was advertised as including 'many advantageous situations for manufactures or other business', it having in particular the advantage of a canal running through the estate [8]. In August 1792 Brooke advertised in *Aris's Gazette* of the speculative aspect of the estate:

> *The takers of land are sure to be recompensed either from a certainty of tenants, in case they are inclined to employ their money in building, or from the annual increase in the value of the land, if taken upon speculation, as is proved by those who have taken lots more than sufficient for their own purpose, having, in the short space of three years, gained, by letting to under tenants, at the rate of from ten to twenty pounds an acre per annum, over and above the rent they pay.*

In order to develop the estate, Brooke borrowed extensively. In May 1789 he obtained £3,000 from Samuel Barnett Esq., a resident of King's Bromley in Staffordshire, and a further £3,181 from a fellow attorney and banker, Charles H. Hunt of Stratford-upon-Avon [9]. In addition to houses for the gentry, Brooke also leased land for the building of houses for the upper working class and tradesmen, on the estate's minor roads. These followed the accepted fashion, adopted by the Gooch and Inge Estates, comprising back-to-back houses, with entries between and yards to the back. The earliest known builder of such houses here was William Windsor, who gave his name to the road he developed. Windsor leased the land from Brooke on 7 April 1790.

It was about this time that the first building societies came into being. The first anywhere in the world was, in fact, in Birmingham. It was established around 1775, by Mr Richard Ketley at the Golden Cross Inn, Snow Hill. It was a small concern, possibly with no more than a dozen or so subscribers. The Northwood Building Society, established at the home of Mrs Sarah Northwood, widow, at The Lamp in Edmund Street, had only twenty members. There are also details of a slightly later society, operating in 1786:

> *…on 11th November, 1782 a Building Company was established at the house of Michael Allen at Hockley to raise a fund to be divided into twenty-one shares and whereas the shares have been balloted for and the said George Thickbroom is entitled to £150 for his three shares…*[10].

With his shares, Thickbroom, a button maker, purchased a house in Walmer Lane. The Amicable Building Society, formed in 1781, required its members to pay subscriptions of 5s a fortnight per share. It was the Society's intention to pay for the building of houses on the Islington Estate of the Rector of Birmingham, valued at between £80 and £140 [11]. Also providing houses here was the Islington Building Society, formed in July 1793, which appears to have deferred the payment of some of its members who took an active part in their construction, such as bricklaying, painting and glazing [12]). At least nineteen building societies were operating in Birmingham during the period 1781-95. They operated as joint stock companies,

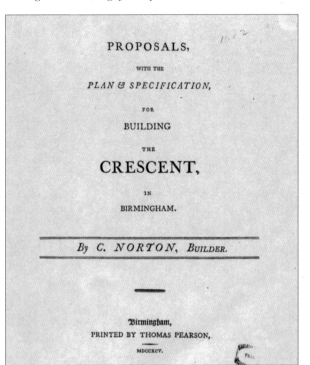

PROPOSALS,

WITH THE

PLAN & SPECIFICATION,

FOR

BUILDING

THE

CRESCENT,

IN

BIRMINGHAM.

By *C. NORTON,* BUILDER.

Birmingham,
PRINTED BY THOMAS PEARSON,

MDCCXCV.

Charles Norton's Crescent speculation, 1795.

Dr.	The Crefcent Scheme for the Buildings.		£.	S.	D.
1795, Sept. 29,	To erecting the fhell of four houfes — —		1180	0	0
1796, March 25,	To finifhing and compleating the above ——		1180	0	0
	To erecting the fhell of four ditto — —		1180	0	0
			3540	0	0
	To balance — — — —		1240	0	0
Sept. 29,	To finifhing and compleating the above four houfes		1180	0	0
1797, March 25,	To erecting the fhell of four ditto — —		1180	0	0
			3600	0	0
	To balance — — — — —		1075	15	0
Sept. 29,	To finifhing and compleating the above four ditto		1180	0	0
1798, March 25,	To erecting the fhell of four houfes — —		1180	0	0
			3435	15	0
	To balance — — — — —		762	0	0
Sept. 29,	To finifhing and compleating the above four houfes		1180	0	0
	To erecting the fhell of two houfes — —		590	0	0
1799, March 25,	To finifhing and compleating the above two ditto		590	0	0
	To erecting the fhell of three houfes — —		885	0	0
			4007	0	0
	To balance — — — — —		1183	15	0
Sept. 29,	To finifhing and compleating the above three houfes		885	0	0
	To erecting the fhell of two ditto — — —		590	0	0
1800, March 25,	To finifhing and compleating the above two ditto		590	0	0
			3248	15	0
	To balance — —- — — —		219	18	9
Dec. 25.	To extras — — — — — —		424	15	7¼
			644	14	4¼

Details and costs for houses in the Crescent.

providing members with their own houses. They rarely built more than fifty houses, and invariably dissolved themselves after the last house had been built and paid for.

There was a trade depression in 1793, following the outbreak of the war against France. Increasingly Birmingham businesses had looked to Europe and more especially France, following the Commercial Treaty of 1786. With this market closed, 500 tradesmen within the town were forced to close down, according to Hutton, with a loss of 10,000 jobs. By 1795 there appear to have been 1,000 houses untenanted in Birmingham [13]. One of the casualties was developer John Brooke, promoter of the Ashted Estate. He became bankrupt in June 1793, with debts of over £3,000. Much of his land remained unleased and plots were still being conveyed after 1816. Yet despite this slump, building continued unabated. In January 1795, some 60 acres of common land lately enclosed in the Parish of Handsworth had been purchased and parcelled out for housing. In this year, 1795, Charles Norton resurrected his ill-fated Crescent scheme, based just off Cambridge Street. The original prospectus had been launched in 1788, but had failed to attract sufficient interest. The new proposal was to build houses valued at £500, by raising subscriptions of £25 per quarter year for every share subscribed to. The money was to be paid into the bank of Taylor and Lloyd. The Crescent was to be an exclusive estate, with no shops or factories permitted. Coach houses and stables were to be erected at the rear, given access by a service road. Norton related in his proposal:

As no other but coaches, or such like carriages, will be suffered to pass in the front of the houses, and as all the land in front will be private property, it is proposed to erect iron gates at each end thereof, to secure the same, and prevent all nuisances and incroachments [14].

The houses were to be built on land leased by the governors of the School of King Edward VI, for a term of 120 years from Lady Day 1790. The houses were to be three storeys in height, with cellars below, and an indoor privy at the rear, the whole to be built of brick, with stone facing. In his initial plan Norton proposed building four houses at a time, which he costed out at £1,180 to construct the shells, with another £1,180 to finish and complete. Unfortunately the scheme was never completed. The four houses at the eastern approach were the only ones constructed. These were eventually demolished in the mid-1960s for the building of tower blocks of flats.

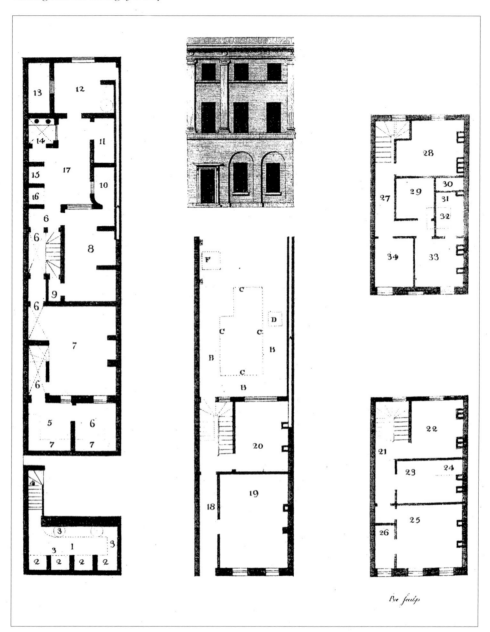

Plan of a house in the proposed Crescent development.

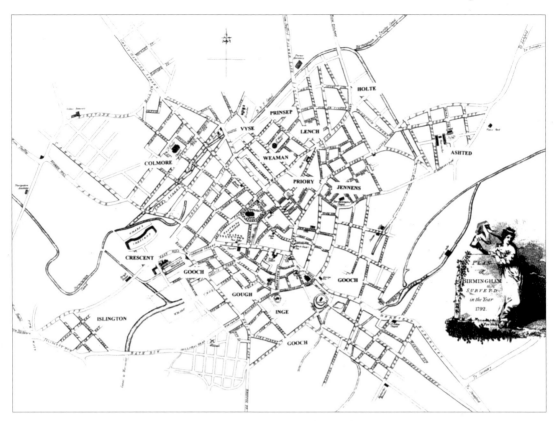

Pye's Plan of Birmingham, 1792: names refer to landowners and developments.

The Crescent.

The Men who Built Birmingham
(1691-1791)

SAMUEL AVERY – bricklayer. Worked with John Collins during 1740s on the Jennens Estate. Built houses in Moor Street 1765.

WILLIAM BENNETT – carpenter and builder. Built houses in the Perry Barr/Great Barr district during 1790s.

BENJAMIN BRETTELL – bricklayer. Laid out and built Brettell Street and other schemes along Snow Hill and immediate neighbourhood.

ROBERT BRIDGENS – carpenter. Worked with Richard Pinley from 1691, building houses for Shem Bracebridge in Phillips Street. Also involved in building some streets on Priory Estate.

THOMAS BULLOCK – bricklayer. Builder in Newhall Street and others on the Colmore Estate, 1761.

JOHN COLEMAN – builder. Developer of Gosta Green and Aston Street, 1780-1790.

JOHN COLLINS – carpenter. One of main builders on Jennens Estate from 1749. Also built individual houses in Birmingham, eg., Park Street, 1740-41.

JOHN CROUDALL – bricklayer working 1690-1697. Associate of Richard Pinley a and builder on the Priory Estate.

JOSIAH DEELEY – carpenter and owner of timber yard in Great Charles St. Worked on the Colmore Estate and in developing the Gooch Estate, 1767 and 1771.

ROBERT GREAVES – builder. Built houses for Northwood's Building Society in 1789. Acted as valuer for William Hutton, following damage to his High Street house in 1791.

ROBERT GRIFFITHS – carpenter. Built houses on the Jennens Estate, pre-1750.

LARKE ENSOR – builder working during 1760s. Partner of Thomas Pinley.

JOSEPH HANDS SR -bricklayer. Erected houses in Colmore Street and later with Richard Pinley and Robert Bridgens, built houses on Priory Estate. Developed Masshouse Lane, off Moor Street.

JOHN HANDS JR – Builder/bricklayer and son of John Sr. Worked in the 1740s and with his father developed Masshouse Lane.

EDWARD HASTIN – builder. Worked on development of lower Gooch Estate around Rea Street, 1786-7.

JOHN HUNT – bricklayer. Built houses in New Street in 1701.

JOHN JENNENS [JENNINGS] – mason. Developed land in Phillips Street in 1691.

JONATHON JOHNSON – carpenter. One of biggest builders in Birmingham in 1730s and 1740s. Worked on individual schemes and responsible for rebuilding the Grammar School and construction of Workhouse.

EDWARD JONES – bricklayer/builder with offices in Snow Hill. Built houses on Colmore Estate and in Great Charles Street,1773. Also built houses in Hampton Street in 1784.

THOMAS LANE – carpenter, 1702-1740. Built houses alongside Richard Pinley in Smallbrook Street and on Priory Estate. Also houses in Edgbaston Street and in The Square.

JOHN LEWIS – bricklayer, 1770-1794. Built houses in Queen Street and Pinfold Street, 1774, Price Street, 1786.

THOMAS NEWCOMB – carpenter, 1691 to 1700.Worked alongside Richard Pinley in development of Phillips Street.

CHARLES NORTON – builder. Worked on several sites. Builder for Northwood's Building Society and architect and builder of ill-fated Crescent scheme, 1789-93.

RICHARD PARKES – Bricklayer/builder in Harborne, c.1740.

WILLIAM PHILLIPS – carpenter of Deritend. Builder on Lower Gooch Estate.

BENJAMIN PINLEY – carpenter/builder. Son of Richard, worked in own right from 1740. Built houses in Gosta Green and Coleshill Street in 1750.

RICHARD PINLEY – (aka Richard Saunders) bricklayer/mason, *c.* 1691–1740. One of foremost builders of Priory Estate. Also involved in earlier schemes; including building houses in Phillips and Colmore Streets, off the High Street.

THOMAS PINLEY – builder. Second son of Richard and partner of Larke Ensor, who were described in an Agreement of 1765 as 'reputable builders'. Developed Snow Hill area.

THOMAS SAUL – builder. Prominent on the Colmore Estate and involved in various smaller developments, 1760, 1763, 1767, 1769 and 1773.

ANTHONY SPICER – carpenter. Built houses on the Colmore Estate, post-1749.

WILLIAM STEPHENS/STEVENS – bricklayer. Son of Joseph Stephens, brickmaker, and builder at Gosta Green. Built two houses which sold for £140 in 1777.

JOHN TONKES – carpenter. Built houses in Moor Street and Stafford Street. Died in 1738.

WILLIAM TAYLOR – bricklayer. Active inYardley area, *c.*1784.

WILLIAM WESTLEY – carpenter and probably most influential builder in early eighteenth-century Birmingham. Designed Priory Estate, was carpenter/builder of St Philip's church and built houses in Temple Row and Dale End. He was working from *c.*1720 and had two sons, William and Richard, who were also builders. The latter built houses in Lichfield Street.

four

The Early Nineteenth Century

To the west of the Rector of Birmingham's Islington Estate, lay the lands of the Gough-Calthorpe family. In 1810 they began laying out their Edgbaston Estate for development. Here it was not a case of development but under-development. This was to be one of the models for the Cadbury's development of Bournville. It was a development driven by quality of life.

Sir Richard Gough bought the Edgbaston Estate, some 1,700 acres, in 1717 for £20,400. He rebuilt Edgbaston Hall, the former home of the old Roman Catholic Middlemore family, and enclosed the grounds surrounding it as a deer park. In 1727 Sir Richard was succeeded by his son Henry, who was created a baronet in April 1728. Henry's son, another Henry, married Barbara Calthorpe of Norfolk in 1742, and in 1796 was created Baron Calthorpe of Calthorpe. In 1788 their son, the second Sir Henry Gough, succeeded to his uncle Calthorpe's estates, on the proviso that he took the family name. He was to be the last member of the family to live at Edgbaston. It was his successor, George, third Lord Calthorpe, along with his land agent, John Harris, who oversaw the development of the Edgbaston Estate.

The first building lease on the Calthorpe Estate had been issued in 1786, for a period of ninety-nine years, with a further eight leases issued by 1796, for plots near Five Ways, between the Hagley and Harborne Roads. In 1791 the Birmingham & Worcester Canal Act was passed. The cut, designed to link Birmingham with the River Severn, passed through the Calthorpe Estate, but unlike Gooch, who embraced the financial possibilities by building wharves and warehouses along the canal that passed through his east Birmingham estate, Calthorpe succeeded in obtaining a clause in the Act, specifically forbidding such construction.

In 1810 Calthorpe and Harris put forward a systematic plan for the considered exploitation of the Calthorpe Estate. The type of tenants they wished to attract were gentlemen and successful tradesmen looking for a small country house set in a spacious garden. Development, it was decided, should continue near Five Ways, and tenant farmers were moved to other parts of the estate in preparation for the cutting of new tree-lined roads, and the parcelling out of this corner of the estate. Between 1812 and 1820, Calthorpe Street, George Street, Frederick Street and Church Street were cut, and plots were surveyed. A second development to the north of the Bristol Road was also set into motion. Wellington, Sir Harry's, Westbourne, Vicarage and Chad Roads were laid out. Under strict supervision, a working-class development was permitted in an enclave east of the Worcester to Birmingham Canal. Sun Street, Spring Street, Balsall Heath Road, Yew Tree Road, and later Varna Road and Princess Road, were cut, and smaller house plots were laid out. By 1836 the Hagley Road from Five Ways to Portland Road had also been fully built up. Between 1810 and 1842, 342 building leases had been issued. Just the other side of Five Ways, just beyond the Calthorpe Estate, in a smaller speculative venture, the triangular piece of land between the Hagley Road and Ladywood Lane was laid out for development with twenty-five plots, and a new road, Francis Road, was cut in 1838. Edgbaston was now irretrievably linked to Birmingham by continued development.

Land and financial assistance was also given by the Calthorpe Estate to charitable institutions, in what was considered a philanthropic approach to the development of the Calthorpe Estate. The Deaf and Dumb Asylum was built in 1814, after being offered favourable terms, as was the Botanical and Horticultural Society in 1836 and the Institute for the Blind in 1851. St George's church was built from 1833, on land given by the family. In addition, in 1853 the estate also leased 8 acres of land in Wheeley's Road as playing fields for the people of Birmingham.

In September 1819 the Calthorpes had further added to their estate by the acquisition of the Curzon Estate, to the south of the Hagley Road. After some negotiation, Lord Calthorpe, upon land agent John Harris' advice, succeeded in purchasing it for £18,500. The only other large Edgbaston estate was the 243-acre Noel Estate, to the west of the Calthorpe Estate, north of the Hagley Road. In 1852 the pen-manufacturing millionaire, Joseph Gillott, acquired it. Though it is certain that he bought it for speculative development, Gillott, a resident on the Calthorpe Estate, was in sympathy with what they were trying to do, and the estate was laid out for development following the Calthorpe model. His estate was developed for the lower middle class and the skilled working class. Its focal point, as in the eighteenth-century estates, was a church, St Augustine's, in Lyttelton Road, just off the Hagley Road. By 1863 substantial houses with good-size gardens, lined both sides of the Hagley Road down to Portland Road. Hagley Road Station on the Harborne Railway was opened in 1874, to serve the district, by which time nearly the whole of north-west Edgbaston had been developed, as had the area around the railway station at Somerset Road, opened in 1876 on the Birmingham West Suburban Railway.

Nearby, east of Monument Road, in Ladywood, development was well underway. By April 1847 Colonel Vyse' Estate, bordered by Ladywood Lane, Icknield Street,

Ledsam Street, St Vincent Street and back to Ladywood Lane, had already been laid out, and new streets cut. Further building continued along Reservoir Road, Icknield Port Road, Beech Street and Icknield Square. A second development in Ladywood was begun on Free School land in 1844, with the cutting of King Edward's Road. This street was largely built up by 1850, as was Nelson Street, Edward Street and Sheepcote Lane. The Ryland Estate, bounded by Sheepcote Street, St Vincent Street and Ledsam Street, was developed from 1848. To serve this growing community, St John's church was built on land leased from King Edward School. The vicar of St George's, Edgbaston, gave £1,000 towards its construction. The church was consecrated by the Bishop of Worcester in 1854, and became a parish in its own right. Two years later a school was erected at the junction of St Mary's and Johnstone Streets.

Meanwhile, back in Birmingham proper, the town had expanded to the north and north-west between 1810 and 1834. Despite a post-war slump after 1815, which affected house building, nonetheless almost 800 houses had been built between then and 1821. Industrial development had occurred around the canal basins off Broad Street and housing had extended to Warstone Lane along Great Hampton Street. In 1805 the estate of the late Joseph Carles situated between Bath Street and the Fazeley Canal was developed and a new street, Shadwell Street, was cut with plots for thirty-four houses. In 1818 Pritchit Street and Bews Street, just north of the Fazeley Canal

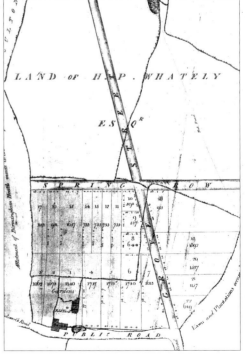

Suburban development of Handsworth, 1808.

were cut, and the land was parcelled out for building on somewhat modest building plots. Also in 1818, that important piece of land in the town centre which made up the triangle between New Street, Ann Street (now Colmore Row) and Temple Street, now became available for development. It was surveyed, and between 1825 and 1827 Waterloo Street and Bennett's Hill were cut and a mixture of domestic, commercial and public buildings were built. The cutting of Bennett's Hill prompted Catherine Hutton to write to her friend, Mrs Buckworth of Tottenham:

Bennett's Hill near Birmingham,
Nov. 26, 1826

My dear Friend,
I say 'near', because an upstart of a street has arisen in Birmingham which has assumed the name of Bennett's Hill. I believe my name and residence are sufficiently known to the post office; but, to make assurance doubly sure, and prevent the possibility of missing a letter of yours, I mention the circumstances…
Catherine Hutton [1]

A somewhat unfair pique by Miss Hutton perhaps, given that the hill's name went back some several hundred years. Even as she wrote from her Washwood Heath home, though, the developing town was expanding towards her, bringing to mind the comic song of Birmingham comedian, Francis Dobbs:

> *I remember one John Growse*
> *A bucklemaster in Brummagem;*
> *He built himself a country house*
> *To be out of the smoke of Brummagem;*
> *But though John's country house stands still,*
> *The town itself has walked up the hill,*
> *Now he lives besides a smokey mill*
> *In the middle of the streets of Brummagem.*

Development continued apace on the edges of the town. Aston Newtown was begun with the development of Asylum Road and Brearley Street in August 1825. One freehold building land surveyors, J.E. & C. Robins, laid out plots varying between 115 and 364 square yards. In April 1854 building continued from Asylum Road towards Six Ways, with the cutting of Alma Street and Inkerman Street, names reflecting the recent Crimean War. To the south of the town, near Camp Hill, the land between Cheapside and Moseley Street, bordering onto the Moseley Road, was laid out in thirty-six plots and offered for auction in February 1824. The middle-class suburb of Ashted was extending north-east to form the new suburb of Bloomsbury, to merge with the populous district of Duddeston by 1834. There was development around the former pleasure grounds of Vauxhall, and by 1837 the

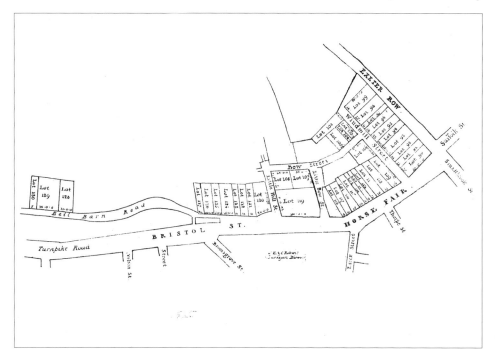

The westward expansion of Birmingham came about with the cutting of the Bristol Turnpike Road.

Grand Junction Railway had reached here. Soon afterwards there were extensive railway works and two gasworks on the other side of the river Rea. Nechells was developed in the second quarter of the century as a working-class district, and by 1841 the population of Duddeston and Nechells was in excess of 20,000. Closer to the town centre, just off Dartmouth Street, south of the Fazeley Canal, soon to be Birmingham MP Joshua Scholefield went into partnership with William Heafield in 1837, to develop a sizeable estate. By March 1838 the land had been divided into 304 building plots, new roads Richards Street, Adam Street and Lord Street had been cut, and several houses were built or were near completion. Elsewhere, the Free School land of King Edward VI, to the west of the Colmore Estate, was parcelled out along Newhall Hill, George Street and Frederick Street, in February 1835. The forty-seven plots had frontages of 11 yards. At the time of its incorporation as a borough in 1838, very little undeveloped space remained in the eastern half of the old parish of Birmingham. With the exception of Soho, the western half was virtually untouched by development. Edgbaston comprised almost half of the undeveloped land lying within the borough, as it was then constituted.

The cutting of a new turnpike road, Bristol Road, was to be the catalyst for change. Building began tentatively in 1825 with a sizeable block of land between Exeter Row and the Horse Fair coming onto the market. Surveyed by J.E. and C. Robins, 130 lots were parcelled out, extending westward along Bristol Street and Bell Barn Road. Beyond this, however, was the Calthorpe Estate, where a more thoughtful approach was given to development. On the other side of the estate, Selly Farm came up for sale in November 1829. Though it was beyond the borough's current boundary, its potential as a residential district, and its easy communication with Birmingham along the turnpike road, was glaringly obvious. The farm, put on the market by J.W. Phipson, was advertised as building land in the sales particulars. Auctioneer, J. Harrison waxed eloquent: 'From its own capabilities and the liberal plans in contemplation for its improvement, promises to become the seat of a neighbourhood, equal, if not superior to Edgbaston itself'. The plots situated along the Bristol Road and Harborne Lane were generous, being 20 yards wide onto the roads, with a depth of 100 yards.

Four years later, in 1835, Selly Hall and its park, situated between the Bristol and Pershore Roads, was offered for sale. Solicitor Robert Dolphin, who later sold 146 acres of the estate to the Counties Benefit Building Society, bought the estate. The Society's intended aim, according to their prospectus, was 'to extend to the middle and upper classes the advantages conferred ... by purchasing large estates in healthy and respectable localities ... and dividing them into lots of not less than a quarter of an acre'. They had the land surveyed and parcelled out, and contracted a builder to cut the roads and install mains drainage. Purchasers were required to spend a minimum of £400 on detached houses, and £350 on semi-detached houses. The name of the estate was changed to the Selly Park Estate and was bounded by Bristol Road to the north, Bournbrook Road, Raddlebarn and Warwards Lane to the west, and Pershore Road to the east. Though the new estate sought to emulate the Calthorpe Estate, all land here was freehold. The Catholic Sisters of Charity later bought Selly Hall from Dolphin in 1864.

The north-western part of the borough, shunned in ancient times for its poor arable land – the area formed today by the districts of Rotton Park, Summerfield, Winson Green, Gib Heath and Brookfields – by the mid-nineteenth century was bisected by canals and railway lines, the very arteries that gave Birmingham life. At first the development here was industrial, with factories and warehouses, but gradually dwelling houses were built nearby to accommodate their workforces. By 1863 the north-western part of the borough, as far as Bachus Road, had been built upon.

Development to the south-east of the town centre began in earnest on 10 August 1829, when three of the owners of estates lying between the Moseley and Pershore Roads in Balsall Heath agreed to provide land for the cutting of a road to link the two turnpike roads together. At a cost of £1,000 and the building of a bridge, Balsall Heath Road was cut. The owner's estates were now made ready for development. The first estate to be laid out was that of William Moore. The Balsall Heath Estate was offered for sale by auction on 2 February 1830. It comprised some seventy-three plots, situated at the junction of the Moseley and Balsall Heath Roads. To serve the new estate, three roads were constructed, Long Bridge Road, Frowd Street (later renamed Sherborne Road, and later again spelt as Sherbourne Road) and Mount Pleasant (renamed Arter Street). In 1838 further development occurred here with the cutting of Haden Street, between Arter Street and the Moseley Road. In the process twenty-eight new plots were created and terraced houses built. On 6 November 1838 the Belgrave Building Estate was parcelled out and offered for sale by auction. This former property of James Wainwright was situated between Sherbourne Road, Seymour Street, Belgrave Road and the Moseley Road.

Following the death of the Revd Vincent Edwards in 1833, the executors of his estate had it laid out for development. Situated west of the Moseley Road, just below Edward Road, the land was offered for sale on 27 June 1834. Two service roads, Tindal Street and George Street, were cut to provide for it. Each plot had a frontage of 22 yards onto the road. Mr Rawlins began building an estate to the east of the Moseley Road, situated between the triangle of Mole Street, Ladypool Road and Highgate Road. Also developed about this time was his land bounded by the Moseley Road, Balsall Heath Road, Mary Street and Cromer Road. The opening of a railway station and the establishment of a horse-drawn bus service in 1846, which plied the Moseley Road six times a day, attracted residents to an area that even then was on the edge of the countryside. Added attractions included a private swimming baths in George Street, opened in 1846, and the Tea Gardens attached to the Orange Tree Tavern. The spiritual needs of the community were addressed in 1853 with the consecration of Balsall Heath's own parish church of St Paul's on the Moseley Road near Highgate Square.

Further land in Balsall Heath, at the junction of Edward Street and Mary Street, was offered for sale in November 1852, and in 1854 further land became available with the construction of Hallam Street. In Sparkbrook, land off Ladypool Road was laid out in March 1853, while nearby the Larches Estate, former home of Thomas Attwood, Birmingham's first MP, came onto the market in December 1856. Finally in August 1857 the last substantial estate in Balsall Heath and Highgate was offered for sale. Leopold, Emily, Dymoke and Angelina Streets were cut. This last development allowed a mixture of housing types, including terraces and back-to-back houses approached through entries. Smaller speculators bought up individual, infilling plots, building anything from one to half a dozen houses, but intermixed with the houses were a number of small factories which, though convenient for local workers, were to cause the dual nuisances of noise and smoke pollution. By 1860, Balsall Heath was fully developed, if not completely built upon.

Beyond Balsall Heath was Moseley village, an isolated hamlet having its origins in Anglo-Saxon times. It possessed a parish church dedicated to St Mary, and two village inns, The Bull's Head near the parish church, and The Fighting Cocks along the Alcester Turnpike. Its houses were clustered around St Mary's. At the time of the 1841 census Moseley had a population of approximately 100. Its populace was mainly engaged in rural employment. There was a wheelwright, blacksmith, a carpenter, farm labourers and a carter. The largest single source of employment though was domestic service. Most found employment at Moseley Hall. As the century progressed some found employment in the homes of successful Birmingham businessmen who had moved to the tranquillity of this north Worcestershire village.

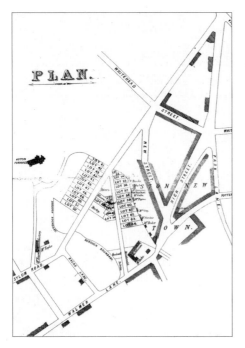

Left: The development of Aston New Town, 1854.

Opposite: The development of Aston, to the north of Birmingham, 1839.

The Andertons, former Birmingham ironmongers, bought up the 596-acre Wake Green Estate, industrialist William Shorthouse bought the twenty-room South Hill House at Greenhill, set in 120 acres of grounds and farmland, and metal merchant Joseph Purden acquired The Henburys, a 45-acre estate which now forms Highbury Park. Smaller houses in and around the village were also built piece-meal. A regular horse-drawn bus service, originating in 1859, and the later railway station opened in 1867, permitted lower middle-class families to commute from the countryside into the town in less than half an hour. By 1872 there were thirty trains a day from Moseley Station to New Street. Modest development in the village began about 1830 when George Johns, a Moseley builder, erected three cottages on the southern corner of Blayney Street. The Blayneys, after whom the road was named, sold off building land from 1843. By 1861 fifteen houses had been built along the street, which by 1891 had been fully developed, and with the construction of a wooden trestle bridge across the railway line, replaced by the present bridge in 1894, had been renamed Woodbridge Road. George Johns appears to have been the builder. He certainly built 14 Woodbridge Road, around 1866, and further along the road he built the Trafalgar Hotel, in 1875.

Following the death of Heneage Legge, Abraham Bracebridge, through his marriage to Mary, the only child of the last baronet, Sir Charles Holte, inherited Aston Hall and Manor. Following poor investments and business failures, Bracebridge was obliged to partition and sell the estate in 1818. Greenway, Greaves & Whitehead, bankers of Warwick, bought Aston Hall and Park. They leased the house and 81 acres to James Watt jr., son of the famous engineer. The rest of the estate was parcelled out

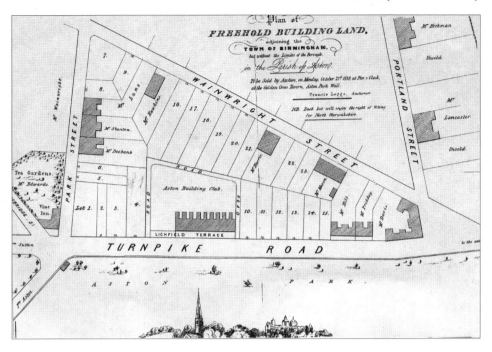

with a view to development. By 1833 some development had already taken place in Aston. To the east of Lichfield Road, around Catherine Street, near Aston Cross, a hamlet had sprung up. There was a small development at Aston Villa, a district named after a mansion on Lozells Lane. The Lozells, on the north-east border of the manor, also supported a small estate. The lower end of Trinity Road, near its junction with Witton Road, had been developed from around 1840, and four streets off Hunters Lane, namely Brougham, Villa and Will Streets and Nursery Row, were marked out for building. In October 1839, the triangle of land lying between the Lichfield Road, Wainwright Street and Park Street had been laid out in plots 12 yards long onto the respective roads. Previously Aston Building Club had erected a terrace of nine cottages along the Lichfield Road here. On larger plots, 24+ yards, individual semi-detached and detached houses had already been built overlooking Aston Park. By 1848 Berners and Guildford Streets were cut, as were Jerome Street (later renamed Gerrard Street) and Wheeler Street, marked out, if not developed. Aston Park Estate itself now became prospective building land.

In 1851, E. & C. Robins surveyed the Park Estate for the Warwick bankers, and laid it out in building plots. This was to be no Calthorpe Estate though. The prospectus of 14 October 1851 described it as being 'suitable for villa and general building purposes'. A quick return on an investment was the motivating force behind this development. The bankers began off-loading plots 12 yards wide for as little as 4s a plot along the Lichfield Turnpike Road. As speculators saw the possibilities, the price was raised to 5s a plot. A new pattern of streets was laid out across the south and east of the former park. Park Road was cut by June 1852, with plots rising from

4s 9d to 6s 3d. Victoria Road, laid out in July 1853, provided a wide, straight main road across half the manor, linking up the Lichfield Turnpike Road with Six Ways. Likewise Newtown was spreading up Summer Row to meet the Park Estate at Six Ways. Beyond here to the north was Birchfield, where creeping urbanisation dates from November 1855. Meanwhile in 1854 a clock tower of brick and stone was erected at Aston Cross, thus giving the Aston Park development a focal point. Land prices rose, as workshops spread into nearby houses, which in turn were demolished for the building of small factories. Tower Road (taking its name from the clock tower) leading off from Aston Cross, was cut in August 1853 and completely laid out and named, if not fully developed, by February 1854, as was Thomas Street and Upper Sutton Street. By 1880 Aston Park Estate had become a seemingly endless sprawl of uniform red-brick tunnel-back terraced houses with Welsh slate roofs. It was a functional estate providing work and housing for the working class and a far cry from the Calthorpe Estate.

five

The Best-Governed City
in the World

Even as Birmingham expanded outwards into the countryside, its town centre was undergoing great change. An Act of Parliament passed into law on 3 August 1846, granted authority to the London & North Western Railway to extend its railway line from Curzon Street Station into the town centre, and there build a station in New Street. Support for the construction of the station came surprisingly from the headmaster of the Free School of King Edward VI who, while not really wanting such a neighbour, preferred it to the existing slum dwellings and inns that currently surrounded the school. The task of building New Street Station commenced with the opening of a short, yet deep open trench, approximately 1 mile in length, running from Curzon Street to New Street. Empowered under the LNWR (Birmingham Extension) Act of 1846, it cost £35,000. Before it could be cut, and the station constructed, a programme for the purchase and demolition of mainly old and dilapidated premises was begun. The land acquired for building included the developments of the late seventeenth-century Froggary, by then a rather unsavoury network of courts and alleys, Peck Lane, Colmore Street and King Street. Also involved was the demolition of a number of religious buildings and the old Prison. Pulling down and almost total rebuilding took seven years and cost over £500,000. This sum included compensation which, when the station was further enlarged in 1882, generated the following piece of social commentary:

A Moving Story

Another place of worship's doomed
A meeting house of mark
And one where Clarke, the parson was
Likewise the parson Clarke
The railway wants for station room
And so it comes to pass,
The Unitarian movement now
Means moving off, alas!

Nor is the chapel only doomed
But graveyard, too, 'tis said,
And Unitarian bodies must
Move off both quick and dead.
Poor souls! That there were laid to sleep
Mid tears of many weepers,
Must now give up their places to
Make room for other sleepers.

The lordly towers of Lawrence there
Now buried 'neath the clay,
The Websters, Bakers, Pembertons,
Must all be moved away.
Dear husbands, sisters, children, wives,
Who long in peace have lain,
And cousins only once removed,
Must be moved again.

Where once the organ rolled and swelled
Where rose the sweet-voiced choir,
The engine whistle now will sound
Perhaps a trifle higher.

Where once a curious service was
Read out or sung in strains,
Another service now there'll be,
A service of quick trains.
'Broad is the way', the preacher said,
'Beware its downward stage';
But broad this new way will not be,
But rather narrow gauge.
'Straight is the road', the preacher said,
'Avoid if you'd shun hell'
But this new road will not be straight,
But curve into a tunnel.

Farewell! Dear dingy Meeting House,
I sigh, alas! To think
That in the chain of history soon
You'll be a missing link.
One Meeting House went years ago,
And now we lose another,
Gentility moved off the one,
Utility the other.

When I am gone take careful thought
Where you will bury me,
Don't stuff me, nor cremate me,
Yet drop me in the sea.
But try a plan that perhaps may bring
Some solid consolation,
Just plant me where a line may come,
And get some compensation.

New Street Station was officially opened for trains both north and south on 1 June 1854. Its tunnels now built, the land above them was offered for sale as building land. Likewise too the Great Western Railway extended its line into Snow Hill, with the same results – demolition and rebuild. It was about this time also, that the early leases on the Colmore Estate fell due. Ann Street and Colmore Row were completely remodelled, as was Bread Street, now renamed as an extension of Edmund Street. The old Georgian houses were pulled down from 1870, and new rows of imposing Victorian buildings erected. New streets were also cut about this time in central Birmingham. The cutting of John Bright Street, at a cost of £31,000, necessitated

Joseph Chamberlain, Mayor of Birmingham (1870-73) and architect of the Improvement Scheme that cleared away the worst slums of central Birmingham.

Laying of water pipes in Waterloo Street, as part of Chamberlain's Improvement Scheme of 1873.

pulling down sixty-eight slum houses and a number of old workshops. Then there was the cutting of Martineau Street, but the most spectacular of all was the cutting of Corporation Street under the Improvement Scheme. This was done during the mayoralty of Joseph Chamberlain, a man with a reputation for transforming dreams into municipal realities. His dynamic administration was also responsible for the provision of gas, municipalising the water supply, the development of a modern sewerage system, the setting up of Board Schools (Chamberlain himself had been one of the prime movers in Forster's Education Act of 1870) and the establishment of administrative departments within the Council to oversee all this progress. Small wonder that American journalist J. Ralph, writing in *Harper's Monthly Magazine* for June 1890, described Birmingham as 'The best-governed city in the world'.

The Improvement Scheme was made possible by the passing of the Artisans' Dwelling Act in 1875. It gave permission to local authorities to compulsorily purchase insanitary areas within the limits of their towns, demolish buildings unsuitable for human habitation and to arrange for new buildings to be erected in their place. What the Act did not allow was the construction by the local authority of working-class houses. Under the Act, the Council secured 43½ acres of land in the centre of the town, namely the old Priory Estate, now degenerated into a rookery of crime and wretchedness, and cleared the area completely. In the process 600

I Can't Find Brummagen

Birmingham comedian James Dobbs (1781-1837) wrote this song and first performed it at the Theatre Royal in New Street in 1828. It tells the story of a man who returns home after an absence of some years to find the town utterly changed.

Full twenty years and more are past,
Since I left Brummagem,
But I set out for home at last,
To good old Brummagem.
But ev'ry place is altered so,
There's hardly a single place I know,
Which fills my heart with grief and woe
For I can't find Brummagem.

As I walked down our street,
As used to be in Brummagem,
I knowed nobody as I did meet,
They change their face in Brummagem,
Poor old Spiceal Street's half gone,
And the poor Old Church stands all alone,
And poor old I stands here to groan,
For I can't find Brummagem.

But 'mongst the changes we have got,
In good old Brummagem,
They've made a Market of the Moat,
To sell the pigs in Brummagem,
But that has brought us more ill-luck,
For they've filled up poor old Pudding-brook,
Where in the mud I've often stuck,
Catching Jack-banils near Brummagem

But what's more melancholy still,
For poor old Brummagem,
They've taken away all Newhall-hill,
Poor old Brummagem,
At Easter time girls fair and brown,
Used to come rolly-polly down,

And show their legs to half the town,
Oh! The good old sights of Brummagem.

Down Peck Lane I walked along
To find out Brummagem,
There was the dungil down and gone,
What no rogues in Brummagem,
They've ta'en it to a street call'd Moor,
T' sign that rogues have got no fewer,
That rogues wont like to go there I'm sure
While Peck Lane's in Brummagem.

I remember one John Growse,
A buckle maker in Brummagem,
He built himself a country house,
To be out of the smoke of Brummagem,
But though John's country house stands still,
The Town itself has walked up the hill,
Now he lives beside a smoky mill,
In the middle streets of Brummagem.

Amongst the changes that abound,
In good old Brummagem,
May trade and happiness be found
In good old Brummagem,
And tho' no Newhall-hill we've got,
Nor Pudding-brook nor any Moat,
May we always have enough to boil the pot,
In good old Brummagem.

Corporation Street, *c.* 1900. Chamberlain's 'Parisian Boulevard', which was cut using the power of the Artisans' Dwelling Act to clear away the worst of the slums.

buildings, including 375 houses, were demolished. Building of the new road, named Corporation Street, began in August 1878. The first stretch, between New Street and Cherry Street, was opened in April 1879. Building sites either side of the new road, as well as land in Cannon Street and Little Cannon Street, and other surplus land, was leased by auction from 9 January 1879. The buildings constructed along these roads were exclusively for commercial purposes. As the leases fell due during the 1970s and '80s, the city regained valuable sites. By 1882 the portion between Bull Street and the Priory, and John Street and Aston Street, was also completed. The cutting of Corporation Street was a long process, not being complete until 1901. In the meantime there was political mischief in the form of harsh criticism of the Corporation for not dealing with the plight of those that suffered from the overcrowding that the scheme had produced:

> *It is little to the credit of the men who have managed the municipal affairs of Birmingham, that not one artisan's dwelling has been built out of the £1,800,000 which has been spent on the new street, and therefore that wretched and unwholesome dwellings, which still remain standing, are overcrowded to a fearful extent.*
>
> *St James Gazette, 1885*

The Chamberlain-controlled Town Council was well aware of this situation. In June 1885 the Improvement Committee prepared a scheme for the building of working-class houses in James Watt Street. £20,000 was borrowed for the work.

The scheme, however, met with political opposition; the same opposition that had condemned them for the original overcrowding. The houses were eventually built by private enterprise. Five years later, in 1889, using the Local Government Board Order of 1883, the Council overcame any opposition and secured a previously undeveloped infill site in a street later called Ryder Street. They built twenty-two two-storey cottages at a cost of £182 per cottage. The houses were completed in September 1890 and were let out at 5s and 6d per week. So successful was the scheme that in the following year they put into action the construction of a further eighty-two houses in Lawrence Street, costing £172 per house. Using the Housing of the Working Classes Act of 1890, in conjunction with the representations of the Medical Officer of Health, the Council was enabled to condemn unhealthy areas and redevelop them. In July 1895 the Council compulsorily purchased a block of properties in Milk Street, Deritend, containing sixty-five houses and workshops. The site was cleared, and upon half of it sixty-four three-room dwellings on a 'dual-house' scheme were built. The upper-storied apartments were rented out at a cost of 3s 9d a week, the lower storey, 4s 4d a week. This very cautious approach to housing the working classes was a compromise resulting from opposing political and capitalist views. Local businessmen argued that it was not the Council's job to house people. The controlling interest in the Council believed that it was. Matters came to a head in 1901; following a close vote (thirty-two to thirty) a Housing Committee was established, taking over all existing powers of the estates and Health Committees, thus enabling the Council to continue with their policy of building council houses for the working classes.

In the suburbs, house-building continued apace. On the edge of the town at Ashted, further building land was released in October 1872 with the cutting of Spooner Street. Earlier, in April 1855, the Nechells Green Estate was surveyed by Samuel Hemmings of Temple Row, and laid out for building on either side of the newly cut William Henry Street, off Rocky Lane. Further down Rocky Lane at Long Acre, on both sides of Charles Arthur Street, the fragmented estate continued.

In 1863, the Victoria Freehold Society of Union Street, Birmingham, developed the Victoria Town Estate, a huge swathe of land in Vauxhall. Its boundaries ran from Duddeston Mill Road in the north, down to and beyond Adelaide Street in the south, bounded in the east by the river Rea, and to the west by Vauxhall Road and Francis Street. Some 158 plots were sold. A further 175 plots were sold by them with the cutting of Alma Crescent, Inkerman Street and Dollman Street. Surveyed by F. Empson, the plots were priced at between 4s 3d and 6s 3d a square yard.

Closer to the town, but out of its smoky environment, on high ground to the east, the suburb of Bordesley was ripe for development. Auctioneer Thomas Fallows offered freehold building land for sale in February 1884. Thirty lots were laid out within the triangle of road between Bordesley Green Road and Green Lane. In the process two new roads were cut, Albert Street and Talfourd Street. At Bordesley Park, leasehold building land became available in June 1885, at newly cut Arthur Street and Bolton Road. In the previous year Bolton Road had been partially built upon, as had Golden Hillock Road. In July 1887 development in Bordesley Park was extended to include the other side of Arthur Street, Cooksey Road and Dixon Road. Further east, ribbon development was begun along Bordesley Green Road in February 1884. That same year the Ward End Estate, just north of the London & North Eastern Railway line, came up for sale. Ward End House was sold off, and its land surveyed for development.

Some ten years later, in September 1894, Batchelor's and Fieldhouse Farms, situated just east of Ward End House, were sold by auctioneer Thomas Fallows as freehold building land. Development continued along the railway line. In fact as early as October 1876, one of the selling features of the Grove Estate, Yardley, was its proximity to Stechford Station. These 16 acres, sold by the executors of Miss Ashmore, stretched from Yardley parish church up to the station. Curiously it was the railway that gave Stechford its name. Formerly, and for several hundred years, it had been Stichford. The careless scrawl of a railway clerk's pen in the naming of its station swept away the ancient spelling.

On the southern edge of the town, infilling took place at Highgate and Balsall Heath. In October 1883, Clevedon Road, not far from the river Rea, was cut and divided up into twenty-six building plots. In 1884 Angelina Street, Dymoke Street and Highgate Street were built up. To the south-west of these two roads lay the Highgate Hill Estate, the last substantial piece of undeveloped land in the area. In June 1884, following the death of Thomas Colmore, the estate was surveyed and laid out by Thomas Fallows along Belgrave Street, Highgate Street, Conybere Street, Angelina Street and Stanhope Street. The estate was offered for auction on 16 and 17 June. By 1890 the last few plots along Balsall Heath Road had been sold.

Beyond the built-up town, encouraged by the proximity of Harborne Station, Grimley & Son offered the 86-acre Ravenhurst Estate, of the late General E.W.D. Bell, for sale as building land on 11 July 1892. Situated just north of the Calthorpe Estate, and south of the Moor Pool Estate, it was a chevron-shaped piece of land bordered by Harborne Railway to the east and Lordswood Road to the west. To the south-east of Harborne, between Moseley and King's Heath, in the triangle of land between Greenhill Road, Cotton Lane and Oxford Road, lay the Greenhill Building Estate. It was sliced up into generous plots, and sold by auctioneers Ludlow & Daniell in April 1871. Its close proximity to King's Heath Station was a major selling point. To lower middle-class families, it was a new life in the country, but with ready access to employment and social life in Birmingham within a twenty-minute train ride. The systematic development of Moseley had begun. The Birmingham Freehold Land Society developed on the other side of Greenhill Road, providing eighty-seven plots and the creation of three new roads: Prospect Road, Avenue Road and Clarence Road. In August 1877 the 596-acre Anderton Park Estate at Wake Green came onto the market. Divided up initially into 100 plots, Anderton Park Road, Stoney Lane, Woodstock Road, Sandford Road, Mayfield Road and Belle Vue, were either newly created or developed to serve what the sales catalogue of the estate described as 'valuable freehold building sites'. An extension of the Greenhill

Estate, Cambridge Road, barely ten minutes walk from the station, was cut, and plots laid out as freehold building land in June 1885. A hundred yards or so to the east of the Greenhill Estate, and just across the road from the Anderton Park Estate, Billesley Lane was also developed from June 1885. Closer to the village, following the opening of Moseley Station, a large tract of building land opposite Moseley Park and Pool, situated along the Alcester Road, became available in June 1886. Just north of the Prince of Wales public house, the land stretched eastwards to Trafalgar Road. Its advertised attraction was that it was just a five-minute walk away from the station. Likewise, taking advantage of the proximity of King's Norton Station, the Newhouse Estate, the property of Mrs S.A. Clarke and Mr J.J. Thompson, and situated at the junction of Westhill Road and Wychall Lane, was offered for sale in May 1889. Each building plot was 24 yards onto the road, falling back to a depth of half an acre.

To the north of Birmingham, from the 1860s to the 1880s development continued at Aston, based around the fringes of the Aston Park Estate. In 1887 the remaining strip of farmland at Aston Brook, just off Aston Road North and situated between Birmingham and Aston, fell to the developers. In July of that year it was laid out in plots, and new roads constructed; Miller Street and Aston Brook Street were cut, and Bracebridge Street, originally developed from 1880 (Nos 30-48, 54-86), was now fully built upon. Holland Road, just before the Aston Cross was cut by 1887, while on the other side of the junction, Catherine Street was fully developed by 1894. The opening of Aston Station in 1862 saw the development of a hamlet, centred on Plume Street, evolve here, and beyond lay Erdington.

The village of Erdington evolved as needs demanded, and life went on at a gentler pace. On the edge of the parish, at Court Lane, eighteen building plots not far from the newly built Oscott College went up for sale in June 1838. On 30 November 1852, further plots along the road, went up for sale, as did land along Gravelly Lane, with a further thirty-six plots on the north side of Short Heath Road. The opening of the London & North Western Railway's Aston to Sutton Line, completed in 1864, offered the skilled working class and the lower middle class, the opportunity of moving out of the industrial town into the countryside, to the north of Birmingham. Development in the Erdington area proceeded at first on a small scale. At the junction of Holly Lane and Bell Lane, twenty-one building plots were laid out for development in June 1871, but in August 1875, very much with commuting in mind, 4 acres of land astride the Sutton Railway, and served by Gravelly Hill Station, were laid for development and auctioned by Birmingham estate agents Roderick & Son. Further land was offered for sale at Lucocks Lane and Fentham Road. At Short Heath, Erdington, Goosemoor Lane was cut up into building plots in July 1881. Arthur Road was cut and developed from April 1894, and during that last decade of the nineteenth century the urbanisation of Erdington continued.

Prior to the opening of Sutton Station in 1864, development here was along the old Chester Road. At Boldmere in April 1860, building land, a modest sixteen plots, came onto the market. By June 1863 this venture was dwarfed when 20 acres of freehold building land at the junction of Chester and Boldmere Roads, was offered at auction. With the coming of the railway Sutton expanded to meet the needs of prosperous Birmingham people who sought homes here. Doe Bank and the Anchorage Estates were carved up into generous house plots. In newly cut Anchorage Road, the thoroughfare was developed into twenty-five lots in July 1870. At the end of May 1871, building land was sold along Rectory New Road. Again generous plots, 22 yards onto the road, were offered. With so many Brummies moving up to here, Sutton had become part of Birmingham, in all but name. Its first mayor, Sir J. Benjamin Stone, was a Birmingham man from Aston. He later became MP for East Birmingham. It was particularly ironic therefore when, 100 years later, the descendants of these Brummies, most of whom could not trace their origins in Sutton beyond two generations, fought tooth and nail, but unsuccessfully, to avoid being taken over by Birmingham in 1974.

By and large these mid- to late- nineteenth-century developments were one-off affairs by speculative builders. One of the great unknown developers of the day was the Birmingham Freehold Land Society. It was a building society founded in 1847, with offices at Nos 42-43 Waterloo Street, Birmingham. They built to suit the suburb, including an incredible number of what were to become known as 'Bye-law houses'. Between 1890-99, they developed nine freehold estates comprising some 294 acres. By 1902 they had developed fifty-eight estates at a cost of £750,000. In the process they created a fair number of new roads. Their sixteenth estate, the Sparkbrook Estate, built in the same year that they developed an estate in Balsall Heath, was situated on land between the Stratford and Warwick Roads. This 277-plot estate was served by five newly created roads, Shakespeare Street, Stratford Street, Sturge Street, Bard Street, and Avon Street. The average plot cost £26 10s 0d. The Balsall Heath Estate situated at the triangle of land between Wenman, Vincent and Hampden Streets, had ninety-eight plots. A further 290 plots were made available by the Society later that year, when they laid out land near Brighton Road Station. This lay between Brunswick and Clifton Roads, butting up to the railway line with newly cut Malvern Street, Balsall Heath. Thomas Fallows later laid out an estate off Brighton Road, extending back to Church Road, and in the process created Newport Road, Pembroke Road and Whitby Road.

Their nineteenth estate was situated at Lozells. Developed in 1856, it was bounded by Guildford Street, Lozells Lane, Wilton Street and Gerrard Street. Fallows & Smith surveyed the land, and each plot was between 199 and 210 square yards in area, selling from between £82 to £87. Further estates followed, mainly terraced 'Bye-law housing', but in 1895 they developed the Middleton Hall Estate, building up the road from a former coach road, and laid out fifty very generous plot sites either side. It was a select development, situated near King's Norton Station, and designed to attract the professional classes. Their forty-second and third estates were on the edge of Edgbaston, the Hagley Road and Stanmore Road Estates. In line with Calthorpe thinking, the promoters insisted that 'No Back Houses, Public Houses, or

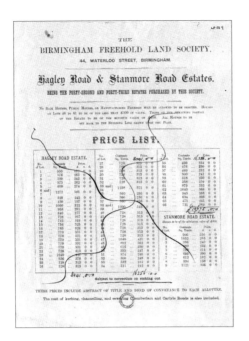

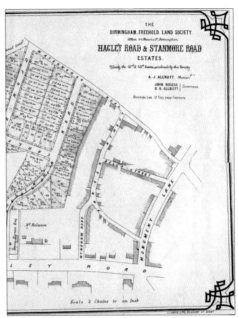

Above left: Birmingham Freehold Land Society: Hagley Road and Stanmore Road Estates.

Above right: Plan of the Hagley Road Estate.

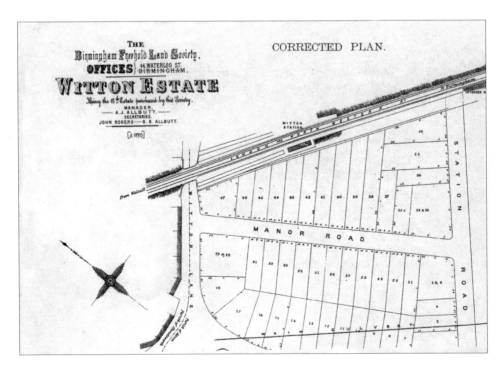

The densely packed Witton Estate, 1880.

Manufacturing Premises will be allowed to be erected. On Lots 48 to 61 to be of not less than £300 in value. Those on the remaining portion of the estate to be of the minimum value of £400'. Sixty-six plots were laid out on the Hagley Road Estate, and two new roads cut, Chamberlain Road (renamed Stirling Road), and Carlyle Road. The Stanmore Road development was a little more modest, comprising a triangle of land at the upper end of the road, onto Portland Road.

The Society's forty-sixth estate was in Handsworth, just off the Wolverhampton Road. Murdock, Linwood, Whatley, Douglas and Albert Roads, were newly cut to serve the 268-plot development. Their forty-seventh estate, the Witton Estate, was developed south-west of the London & North Western Railway, and serviced by Witton Station. It had forty-seven plots, most of them with frontages of 12 yards to the road. Serviceable, but very different to the Hagley Road development, it consisted of monotonously constructed terraced houses. When the Warley Abbey Estate, former home of the Galton family, came up for sale in 1901, the Freehold Land Society purchased a sizeable plot bounded by Lightwoods Road and Three Shires Oak Road. Across the road Birmingham City Council bought land, and further along, Barnsley & Sons, the firm of well-known developers, acquired the remainder. The Society spent £953 in road making on their section of the estate, having laid it out for 2,000 houses, 'suitable for the artisan and lower middle classes'. In 1903 they bought an estate at Ward End, close to the city: Ward End House and Park. The park, just over 200 yards away from the Society's development, was opened as a civic amenity, greatly enhancing their estate. This notion of superior working-class houses in generous plots, ideally set down in parkland or countrified surroundings, already had a precedent with the Cadbury Brothers' development at Bournville.

six

Bournville and Moor Pool

The Bournville Estate, so long looked upon as a great experiment in social housing, was first and foremost driven by practical commercialism. Right up to the 1950s, that other great Birmingham food producer, Birds, of custard fame, advertised their factory as being at 'Deritend, near Birmingham, on the banks of the river Rea'. In reality it was in the heart of the industrial city. The Cadbury Brothers, Richard and George, were astute enough to realise that to promote their product as being pure and wholesome, it would benefit from appearing to have been manufactured in a clean and healthy setting, namely the countryside. This point was subsequently taken up in their advertising, where the Bournville works are described as 'The factory in a garden'. The green site that they found in 1878 was situated near Selly Oak, and importantly was serviced by the Birmingham & West Suburban Railway and the Worcester & Birmingham Canal. The problem that the brothers faced was that their workforce lived in Birmingham. At first the firm negotiated with the railway company to provide cheaper fares for its workforce on the basis of a guaranteed number of commuters per day. As finances stabilised following their move from Bridge Street to Bournville, the company began building cottage homes for their senior foremen. Fifteen semi-detached houses, designed by George Gadd, were built near the factory from 1879.

In 1895 the Bournbrook Hall Estate, adjacent to the factory, was purchased to allow for expansion. Two years prior, the concept of a garden village now very much in mind, George Cadbury secured further adjoining land to prevent speculative builders from developing it. Bournville Building Estate was established in 1893, and A.P. Walker was appointed its first architect. The village Cadbury envisaged was not originally designed to house his ordinary workforce. The prospectus specified that none of the houses should be below a certain size, and should cost a minimum of

George Cadbury, visionary founder of the Bournville Estate.

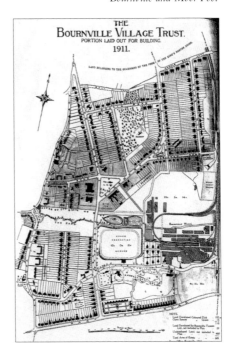

Plan of the Bournville Estate, 1935.

£150 to construct, in order to attract a 'superior class of quiet and respectable tenant'. Cadbury was constructing a village for the middle classes and skilled artisans, and not for the majority of his own employees, as the Bournville myth contends. In 1895 the brilliant young Birmingham architect, William Alexander Harvey, was appointed estate architect at Bournville. His Arts and Crafts-style cottages gave the village its distinctive 'Bournville style' of red brick, rough cast and half-timber, with pan tile or green slate roofs. By 1900 the estate covered 330 acres and 300 houses had been built. It had been Cadbury's intention to sell the sites and cottages outright, and thus create a class of small freeholders. The problem arising from this was that there was no guarantee that the new owners would maintain their homes in harmony with their neighbours. So instead the estate decided to sell the houses, but leasehold the land for a term of 999 years, charging ground rent. More importantly, clauses and covenants were inserted to maintain the harmony that the estate's builders so desired. The Bournville Building Estate now began issuing mortgages to those who had not sufficient capital to purchase houses outright. Some time later cottages were rented out to tenants, thus enabling the better-paid Cadbury employees the opportunity of living near to their work. By 1903, less than half of the householders on the estate worked at Cadbury's. It was not until the establishment of the Bournville Works Housing Society, made up of Cadbury employees, that the workforce could afford to live here.

Most of the cottages built before 1901 had three bedrooms, with two sitting rooms, a scullery and a toilet. Some of the larger houses had an extra bedroom and a bathroom, supplied with hot and cold water. By 1903, smaller cottages for

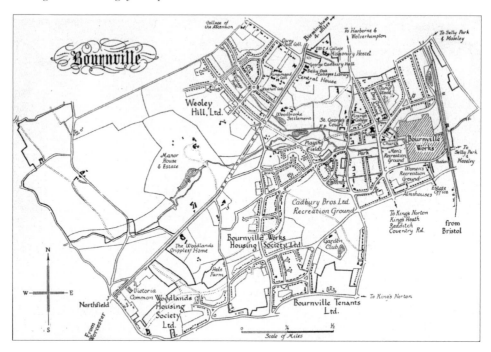

The expansion of the Bournville Estate, 1935.

rent had just two bedrooms. Rents varied from 5s 6d to 12s a week. Gas and water supplies were served by Birmingham. The average garden space allowed for these early houses was 600 yards, and estate gardeners initially laid out the gardens. Lines of fruit trees – pear, apple and plum – were planted to provide fruit, and to form a screen between the gardens for privacy. In addition to the gardens the estate also provided some 200 allotments.

On 14 December 1900, the Cadbury's handed over the administration of the estate to a body of trustees, the Bournville Village Trust (BVT), of which George Cadbury was chairman. This gift was valued at £200,000 and consisted of 458 acres and the village of Bournville, of which in 1903 just 100 acres had been laid out for building. Cadbury's ideals formed the basis of their charter. The Foundation Trust Deed laid down that the houses were not to be crowded on the land, but that each was to occupy not more than one quarter of its own site. Factories were not to occupy more than one fifteenth of any developed area. One tenth of the land, in addition to roads and gardens, should be devoted to parks and recreation grounds. There should be ample space between the rows of cottages and the roads should be planted with trees. Sites should also be made available for public buildings. The aim of the Foundation Trust Deed was to preserve the rural character of the village, and to provide a healthy environment for its inhabitants. The transfer to the BVT saw an end to the 999-year leases. The Trust wanted to retain ownership and control over its houses. Already many of the original owners of these properties had sold their houses and in many cases for a good profit.

The village green, Bournville (BVT guide).

The Woodlands Estate, Bournville (BVT guide).

The Men Who Built Birmingham
(1800-1900)

JOHN. BARNSLEY & SONS

Large company with national reputation, employing between 500 and 1,000 workers. Barnsley, former employee of Matthew Boulton, founded firm in 1826, originally in Broad Street, but later in Ryland Street. Sons, Thomas and Edward, were friends of architect John Henry Chamberlain and erected many private houses and business premises to his designs, and became partners in father's business in 1885. The Barnsleys introduced Gothic architecture to the city and commissions included the Council House, the Museum and Art Gallery and General Hospital. Collaborated with Chamberlain and William Martin building Board Schools. Built churches and chapels in Birmingham and municipal buildings throughout England and Wales. In London the Drapers' Hall in Throgmorton Street and St Michael's church in Cornhill. At the turn of the century, C.H. and John Barnsley took over the company from their fathers.

JOHN BOWEN

Firm's offices in George Street, Balsall Heath. Developed estates in Balsall Heath and Moseley, built the Central Hall in Corporation Street and St Agatha's church, Sparkbrook, the Law Courts in Corporation Street (1891), the Birmingham Meat Market, the Corporation Baths in Monument Road and Hollymoor Asylum. Bowen was president of Birmingham Master Builders Association in 1884 and made President of the National Federation of Building Trade Employers of Great Britain and Ireland in 1894. He was an alderman and JP and in 1916–17 was High Sheriff of Worcestershire.

SAMUEL BRIGGS

One of the largest builders and contractors in the area, involved in various developments in and around Birmingham from 1845. He was first chairman of the Balsall Heath Local Board and one of the directors of the Midland Land Corporation.

EDWARD JOHN CHARLES

Chief assistant to John Bowen leaving in 1892 to form his own company with offices at Thelsford Works, Moseley. By 1900 he was employing 350 men and the firm was building offices and model houses on Cadbury's Bournville Estate. He was involved in large-scale developments in Sutton Coldfield, built the new Mermaid Hotel in Sparkbrook, The Fighting Cocks Hotel, Moseley, the City Arcades and The Imperial Theatre.

WILLIAM CHARLEY

Offices were at Vaughton's Hole, Balsall Heath. Developed the last part of the Haden Estate in Balsall Heath, building 55 houses and 9 shops. The firm also built the Brighton Hotel and Belgrave Hotel in 1875.

JAMES DRAISEY

Speculative builder in the Highgate-Balsall Heath area who was responsible for developing a number of streets there in the late nineteenth century.

FREDERICK GOWING

Offices in Belgrave Road, Balsall Heath. Building contactor on a large scale, working on private and City Council projects

GRANT'S ESTATES

Offices were at 1791, Pershore Road, Cotteridge. Henry Michael Grant, after being apprenticed to building trade in Leicester in 1880, became foreman to George Johns of Moseley. In 1887-8 he formed own company with brother Thomas. They built terraced housing blocks around Cotteridge and King's Heath and jobbing building work, while establishing a reputation. By 1907 they had built the Cotteridge Estate, at a cost of £171,000, the Grange Estate, King's Heath (£49,000), Grant's Bournville Estates (£254,000), Selly Oak Estate (£71,000), Selly Park Estate and Pebble Mill Estate (£405,000) and Sir Josiah Mason's Orphanage Estate, Erdington (£146,000). The company remained in business until 1961 when it was taken over by Sewell's.

JAMES KENT

A leading speculative builder in the city, deriving his capital from his boot trade. Worked with Thomas H. Bott of Stechford, on developments in the Yardley and Stechford area.

WILLIAM SAPCOTE

Offices were in Camden Street, Ladywood. The firm was founded by William Sr and the by his son, William Jnr, whose brother Richard later joined the firm too. As well as building houses, and Board Schools, they were responsible for building the Municipal Technical School in Suffolk Street, St John's church, Sparkhill, the Electric Power Station in Summer Lane and the Telephone Exchange in Hill Street.

The men who built late nineteenth- and early twentieth-century Birmingham. Clockwise from top left: Fredrick Gowing, John Bowen, Thomas Barnsley, John Rogers.

The original village was laid out with roads 42 feet wide, and all were planted with trees. Full advantage was taken of the undulating and well-wooded site to give pleasant variety to the layout of the estate. Banks and curves in the road were planted with shrubs and flowers. Wherever possible the original trees and hedgerows were preserved. A village green with a rest house at its centre was constructed. An Elementary School to the west of the green was built in 1905. Near the school, Ruskin Hall, later to become the Bournville School of Arts and Crafts, was built as a social and intellectual centre. To the north of the green a Friends Meeting House was constructed and, almost adjoining, a Day Continuation School. On the south side of the green Bournville church, dedicated to St Francis, was built, as were a number of village shops. There were to be no public houses or off-licences though. Clause 33 of the Foundation Trust Deed stated, 'No house or building shall be used for such sale except under the following conditions. That the unanimous consent in writing of all the Trustees shall be necessary...' As a Quaker, Cadbury was firmly committed to the Temperance movement and firmly believed that alcohol was a dangerous agent of destruction for the labouring poor. Cadbury's attitude to alcohol consumption though was not without some hypocrisy – the account books of Birmingham wine merchants Connolly & Olivieri reveal that George Cadbury was one of their biggest customers!

The very size of the Bournville Estate meant that it would have been financially impossible to develop the estate using the BVT's own resources. It therefore adopted a policy of leasing land to co-partnership housing associations. The first was Bournville Tenants Ltd, who leased 20 acres of land in 1906 for a period of ninety-nine years. For every 10 acres leased, the Trust gave 1 free acre for the provision of open spaces. The association built 146 houses to designs by Bournville's architect, W.A. Harvey. They also constructed a village hall to serve the community on the gifted 1-acre site. In 1914 Weoley Hill Ltd leased land north of the Bristol Road. In the post-First World War period they built 348 houses and bungalows, eventually rising to 500 after 1935. The Bournville Works Housing Society Ltd devoted solely to Cadbury employees, leased land from the Trust. By 1935 they had constructed over 360 houses. In a truly socialist move for the time and not typical of George Cadbury himself, these houses were let to married couples with young families living in overcrowded accommodation. The fourth organisation to lease land for development was the Woodlands Housing Society Ltd, which built houses on the south-westerly part of the Bournville Estate. In 1950 the BVT leased further land to Cadbury employees who had banded together to form Hay Green Housing Association. They constructed twenty-four bungalows. In all twenty-eight self-build associations leased land from the Trust. In 1993 the BVT sold the last substantial building site on the Bournville Estate to the private development company George Wimpey plc, who developed the site in conjunction with Berkeley Homes.

In the Birmingham of 1907, Chairman of the Housing Committee, John S. Nettlefold, acknowledged public demand that the city's slums should be cleared away. To compulsorily purchase these areas and redevelop them would have been

J.S. Nettlefold was a prime mover in the success of Harborne Tenants Ltd.

prohibitively expensive. Further to his argument, he cautioned that if these areas were to be cleared all at once, it would create a housing famine for the working class. The Conservatives on the City Council advocated that the city should replace the 'back-to-backs' with Liverpool-style flats. Others advocated the Council buying up slum courts and improving them. Nettlefold was against both proposals.

Municipal flats were tried in a development in Milk Street, but they looked just like army barracks, and did nothing to relieve congestion. The cost of replacing slum housing necessitated the raising of rents beyond the means of working people to regain the investment. His initial response was to relax policy on existing slum areas, insisting that it was the responsibility of the owners of insanitary housing to bring them up to the requirements of public health, at their own expense – ratepayers should not be expected to pay.

Nettlefold argued that it was just as important to prevent the creation of new slums as it was to renovate old ones. The only answer to the housing crisis in the city centre was to decentralise the population to the suburbs. Nettlefold, an active member of the Garden City Association, was a firm believer that suburbanisation was the role of private enterprise, and here he looked to Bournville as his model. During his chairmanship of the Housing Committee he loosened building bye-laws to stimulate the investment in private developments by reducing building costs, improving roads and extending the tram system in order to facilitate suburban development. His opportunity to show the commercial viability of providing a working-class housing estate, offering house rents within the means of the poor, while offering a healthy return to investors, came when he was invited to become chairman of Harborne Tenants Ltd.

The building of Moorpool Avenue on the Moorpool Estate by Harborne Tenants Ltd.

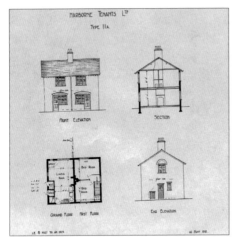

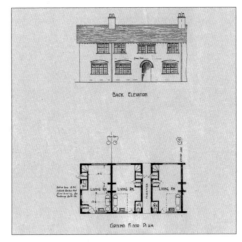

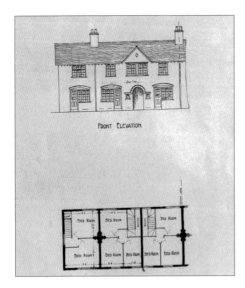

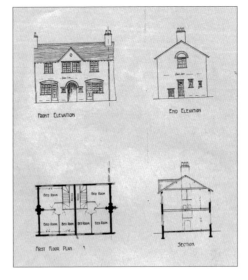

Plans and drawings of Harborne Tenants Ltd.

In the autumn of 1906 a proposal to construct a tramway between Birmingham and Harborne was placed before Parliament. Undeveloped land at Harborne rose in price as a consequence. A Co-partnership Tenants Society, committed to constructing a garden suburb, put in a bid for the 36-acre Moor Pool Estate. The owner rejected it.

However when the Tramway Bill failed in Parliament, land prices fell, and the co-partnership eventually succeeded at their second attempt. A meeting was called of the promoters and prospective tenants under the chairmanship of J.S. Nettlefold and Mr Crossley Greenwood of the co-partnership. It was decided to buy up an adjacent 18-acre plot, which gave access to a main road on the Birmingham side of the estate, just a short distance away from Harborne Station. The cost of the now 54-acre estate, with its transport access to Birmingham, was £15,860.

The Society registered as Harborne Tenants Ltd, and was established to promote the erection, co-operative ownership and administration of houses on the Moor Pool Estate. Its stated aims were:

> *To erect substantially-built houses, provided with good sanitary and other arrangements, for the convenience of tenants. To let the houses at ordinary rents; to pay a moderate rate of interest on capital; and to divide the surplus profits (after providing for expenses, repairs, depreciation, etc.) among the tenant members, in proportion to the rents paid by them. Each tenant member's share of profits is credited to him in shares instead of being paid in cash, but any tenant member who has invested an equal amount equal to the value of the house he occupies will be entitled to receive his share of the profits in cash.*

In October 1907, Mrs J.S. Nettlefold cut the first sod. In attendance was Dr Gore, first Lord Bishop of Birmingham. He gave a short address acknowledging that they:

> were perfectly conscious that the housing problem lay at the very root of social reform. There must be better houses, more air, more gardens, and more open spaces for playgrounds for the children. The Harborne Tenants Ltd, aspired to provide houses under these conditions within the means of workmen and artisans.

Building commenced on 1 January 1908 to housing designs by Mr F.W. Martin of Martin & Martin of No. 106 Colmore Row, Birmingham. By 1909, 230 houses had been built and rented out at between 4s 8d and 11s per week, not including rates. In the relaxation of bye-laws proposed by Nettlefold, the roads were laid out 16 feet wide, with a broad band of grass, planted with trees either side, and gravel pathways between the grass and gardens. The trees, mountain ash, silver birch and thorn were planted upon the advice of Mr Thomas Humphreys, curator of the Botanical Gardens. Hedges of beech were planted between each garden to give privacy. The gardens were not so big as those of Bournville, but were designed such as the average working man could keep in order in his spare time. For the keener gardener allotments were provided. A park was laid out around the Moor Pool, as well as a number of small playgrounds for the children. A lawn tennis court was later provided and a social clubhouse built.

There were critics of both Bournville and Moor Pool. Both Nettlefold and Cadbury were accused of having produced 'Arcadian retreats' which could be afforded only by better-paid working people and the middle classes. Unionists on the Council sneered that the relaxation of town planning would create 'suburbs of smug respectability for the aristocracy of labour'. To a degree it was true, and following a radical re-think, it was to be the City Council itself that was to produce affordable working-class houses set in well-planned countryside estates.

seven

The Long Summer
1900-1914

In the twenty-year period from 1891 to 1911, Birmingham expanded beyond all recognition to become the second city of the United Kingdom, overtaking Glasgow in the process. In 1891 Harborne, Balsall Heath, Saltley and Ward End came into the city. In 1909 Quinton, a much-neglected corner of Worcestershire, upon its own request, was admitted into Birmingham. Under the Greater Birmingham Act of 1911, Handsworth (reluctantly), Aston Manor and Erdington became part of Birmingham. The equally neglected Worcestershire parishes of Yardley, King's Norton and Northfield were absorbed too, despite a late attempt by Worcester County Council to upgrade Yardley to urban district status, with its own council houses along the Stratford Road at Sparkhill. By 1905 these suburbs were populated by people who looked to Birmingham, rather than Worcester, for their medical care, lighting, gas, water supply, sewerage and, of course, transport by tram or train into the city.

The growth of Birmingham from 1911 to 1914 was one of gradual expansion and infilling. Land use changed from agricultural to urban as the ever-growing population moved to the suburbs to escape the pollution of the inner city. New land became available as and when it was required. Yet it was not until the late 1960s that the last plot of undeveloped land, within the 80 square miles of the then city, was finally developed for residential or industrial purposes.

At the time of its inclusion into Birmingham in 1911, Aston, with a population of 329,798, was already seamlessly joined in its urban development to the city. The General Electric Company between 1899 and 1901 bought up the last major piece of undeveloped land at Witton, building a factory and houses for its employees in the tract of land between the railway line north-east of Aston Park and the Tame Valley Canal. To the north-east, Erdington remained largely undeveloped until the beginning of the railway age. There had been some development in the early part of the nineteenth century around Gravelly Hill, but the opening of Gravelly Hill and Erdington Stations in 1862 resulted in extensive building around each. By 1900 the main road between the two stations was fully built up, and development was continuing westward into Stockland Green and Short Heath, and to the east towards Moor Green. At Wylde Green, freehold building land was released for development, while a further 4 acres of freehold building land adjoining Oaklands at Doe Bank, the estate of the late Harry Rudder, also came onto the market. At Four Oaks, freehold building land at Blackroot Road, Mere Green Road and several other roads recently laid out came onto the market in July 1914. The 200-acre Four Oaks Estate had formerly been a racecourse, situated 1 mile north of Sutton Coldfield town centre. Its then owner, the Marquis of Clanricarde, divided it up into very generous development plots in 1890. Even as late as 1931, housing density was still only four houses per acre. The estate was bounded by the Lichfield Road to the north, Four Oaks Road, Sutton Park and Blackroot Road, and was administered by the Four Oaks Company Ltd, who laid out and maintained the roads and pavements, and controlled new development. Large houses, generally two to three storeys in height, were built here in heavily wooded and well-screened grounds of up to 3½ acres. The roads were lined with regularly spaced lime trees set in informal grass verges. What made the estate special was the quality of the early house design. Architecturally, a large proportion of these houses were designed for prosperous Birmingham families by noted Arts and Crafts movement architects, including W.R. Lethaby, Ernest Newton, C.E. Bateman, A.S. Dixon, Edwin F. Reynolds, J.L. Ball, W.H. Bidlake and Crouch & Butler.

The 81 acres of Batchelors Farm Estate in Belcher's Lane, lying conveniently between Bordesley Green tram terminus and Stechford railway station, became available for development in July 1910. The estate extended eastwards towards the river Cole, which in itself was a further selling feature. The Birmingham Freehold Land Society developed some twelve streets near Ward End Park during this period, and the development of the Wolseley motor car factory at Washwood Heath and the construction of the Metro-Cammell Works nearby, saw the extension of residential districts in this part of the old parish of Aston. At Small Heath 60 acres of building development land between the Coventry Road, the river Cole and Oldknow Road up to the railway line near the BSA factory was laid out in plots and offered for sale by auctioneers Knight, Frank & Rutley on 9 July 1913.

By 1910, three railways cut across the parish of Yardley: the LMS, GWR and the North Warwickshire Railway. They gave access, and to a large degree were responsible for, the urban development of Yardley. Their stations, including Stechford, opened in 1844. Acocks Green (1852), Spring Road (1919), Tyseley (1906), Hall Green (1908) and Yardley Wood (1908) all facilitated the urban development of the old parish. For a long time before its 1911 inclusion into Birmingham, Yardley had been a favourite residence for Birmingham businessmen. By the 1880s industrial sites had also developed at Hay Mills, Greet and Stechford, and, serviced by trams and buses, working-class districts had sprung up at Sparkhill and Sparkbrook.

Above left: The break-up of the Severne Estate in Hall Green released 419 acres for development.

Above right: Providing houses at Longbridge ensured the expansion of motor car production.

Acocks Green had developed from 1852 with the opening of its railway station. By 1900, when the Acocks Green House Estate land was offered for sale, the suburb had become a mixed middle-class and working-class neighbourhood, pushing northwards with its development to South Yardley, to be met by the eastward expansion of Hay Mills along the Coventry Road. Also by 1900 Stechford was linked to Yardley by urban development, extending down Stoney Lane and Church Road to the Coventry Road, also to be joined by the terraced housing of the working-class district of Hay Mills.

The old hamlet of Hall Green had originally developed around the Bull's Head, just off the Stratford Road, reaching back towards Job Marston's chapel, later to become the Church of the Ascension. By 1908 building had continued on the other side of the Stratford Road and, by speculative developments, reached down Highfield Road to Yardley Wood Station. Meanwhile development also continued along the Stratford Road adjacent to Hall Green Station. At Baldwins Lane, in a small speculative venture, building land was offered for sale in January 1909. Larger estates too were coming onto the market. Agents Grimley & Son sold the Trittiford Estate at Yardley Wood on 25 June 1903. It consisted of land between Highfield Road and Scribers Lane, from the river Cole reaching up almost to Robin Hood Lane.

In 1912, the 419 acres of the Severne Estate, described in the sales catalogue as 'Building land ripe for immediate development', was offered for sale at the Grand Hotel in Birmingham by auctioneers Knight, Frank & Rutley. Included in the sale was Hall Green, three farms, Hall Green racecourse and the Robin Hood golf course. The property, not fully developed until the 1930s, consisted of land along the Stratford Road, School Road and Church Road to the south, and Fox Hollies Road to the east, with further land along Lakey Lane, Shirley Road, and long frontages to Robin Hood Lane and Highfield Road. It joined onto the Trittiford Estate, likewise not really developed until the 1930s. The selling point of both estates, apart from being prime development land, was their easy communication with the city. The Severne Estate lay astride the proposed extension of the Birmingham Corporation's Electric Tramway System along the Stratford Road. In addition both Hall Green and Yardley Wood Stations also serviced it. In July of the following year, the Cole Bank Estate was offered for sale, but in comparison to the Yardley Estate of A.J. Taylor, also offered for sale that same month, it dwarfed into insignificance. The Yardley Estate was a huge swathe of land, 648 acres, ranging from Hall Green Station in the north, down to Yardley Wood Station in the south and beyond, down to the Stratford-upon-Avon Canal. The estate consisted of building land ripe for immediate development, with five big farms, Sarehole and Trittiford Mills, accommodation land and cottages. Additional land was also available at Stirchley. The plots were laid out by land agent R. Edward Couchman, and offered for sale by auctioneers Knight, Frank & Rutley. By the outbreak of the First World War, Hall Green had been parcelled out, if not fully developed.

By 1900, development in Moseley was mainly one of infilling. Expensive houses were being built that, even though they increased density, nonetheless, because of their quality, did not destroy the social standing of the suburb. In the first decade there were one or two outstanding middle-class developments here. Moor Green Estate, land fronting Yew Tree Road and Queensbridge Road, just over 11 acres, was auctioned for development by Edward, Son & Bigwood on 12 December 1912. Harking back to Birmingham's eighteenth-century developments, with a church as its focal point, was the Wake Green Estates of Messers Willmot. The estates were offered for sale by two firms, Grimley & Son, and Thomas & Betteridge, on 11 July 1903. A spinal road, St Agnes Road (taking its name from the church), was cut through the estate linking it to Wake Green Road and Stoney Lane. Oxford Road was continued from Billesley Lane, to meet up with St Agnes Crescent. Fifty-two plots were initially offered for development with covenants as to how much must be spent on the houses built upon them. Naturally the plots nearest the church had the highest specification; £900 for detached, £850 for semi-detached. These were generous plots of almost 2,000 square yards, with frontages of 24 yards onto the road. Today the area is noted for its high quality of architecture, much of it showing the development of the Arts and Crafts movement in Birmingham. There are houses by Charles Edward Bateman, W. DeLacy Aherne, father of film actor Brian Aherne, J. Brewin Holmes and James & Lister Lea, architects of the magnificent Barton Arms in Aston. The estate is justifiably now a conservation area.

South of Moseley, at King's Heath and beyond, some few streets were cut, and a new estate was established at Hazelwell, which was provided with its own railway station as a consequence. Nearby, in 1913-14 Cartland and Newlands Roads were cut. Elsewhere, housing gradually crept along the road at Brandwood, between Alcester Lanes End and King's Norton. Stirchley, where building had begun in earnest from 1848, continued to expand along the Pershore Road until it linked up with Cotteridge, creating a linear village, served by Lifford and King's Norton Stations.

In November 1905, Herbert Austin opened his car manufactory at Longbridge. By 1914 he had 2,000 employees. Earlier, in May 1909, Eli Sidwell released 10 acres of land along Bristol Road South for development. Divided into thirty-three plots, the land was designed for working-class housing. Austin workers no doubt bought some of them, but this was a speculative small venture. With the outbreak of war, production at Longbridge moved from cars to the manufacturing of armoured cars and aeroplanes. Initially Austin ran a fleet of thirty buses to get his workforce from Birmingham to Longbridge. With the expansion of the factory Austin took on extra workers. Commuting became more difficult; some workers were obliged to walk 4 or 5 miles a day to work. As an alternative to commuting, Austin decided to build a village for his employees. He bought a new site of freehold land from Thomas Middlemore for £7,750 and laid out roads and sewers. Gaining a relaxation in planning regulations from Birmingham Council, Austin then sent off to the American, Aladdin Company of Bay City, Michigan for 200 prefabricated bungalow kits. The red cedar bungalows, despite the threat from U-boats, arrived safely. The bungalows, interspersed by twenty-five pairs of conventional, brick-built houses to act as fire-breaks, were all erected within eleven months. In a manner reminiscent of the Bournville village, mature trees on the site were incorporated into the scheme; limes, scarlet chestnuts and planes were planted along the major roads, and rowans, maples and cedars along the minor roads. When completed, Longbridge workers occupied the bungalows and houses; seven per bungalow, twelve per house. Five roads, Hawkesley Crescent, Hawkesley Drive, Central Avenue, Coney Green Drive and Cypress Way, served the estate. At the end of the war as contracts petered out, Austin was obliged to lay-off much of his workforce, and the bungalows were vacated. They were readily taken over by families desperate for houses. The estate still exists, and is also now a conservation area.

The last bits of Edgbaston, beyond the Calthorpe Estate, were all developed in the decade leading up to the outbreak of the First World War. The last of the freehold building land along City Road and Clarendon Road was developed during 1911. The Rotton Park Estate, former Gillott Estate land, was offered at auction in June 1911. It was largely infill land along the Hagley and Fountain Roads, Gillott Road, Melville Road, Clarendon Road, Vernon Road, Portland Road, Selwyn Road, Wheatsheaf, Bernard Road and Rotton Park Road. Grant's Estates continued to develop in the Selly Oak area. In 1905 they built a new estate called The Avenues. It consisted of five avenues of terraced houses. The first six houses in First Avenue were completed by November 1905. A small number of double-fronted houses were built on the corner sites of Fourth Avenue and St John's Road.

In addition to the development of the Harborne Tenants Association at Moor Pool from 1907, a second, 200-acre plot on the Lords Wood Estate was also developed at the same time, and the land between it and Harborne Heath was also being progressively built up. At the southern end of Handsworth parish, also formerly part of Staffordshire before its inclusion into Birmingham, there was progressive development of quality housing along the Birchfield Road, Heathfield Road and Holyhead Road. Land at Church Vale, near the parish church, was released as building land in April 1889. The existence of Perry Barr and Handsworth Stations encouraged the northward and westward expansion of the parish. The land between Birchfield Road and the Aston Park Estate was filled during the decade by working-class housing. During the period 1900–14, 35,061 houses were built in Birmingham.

In the spring of 1913 the City Corporation set up an enquiry to investigate the housing conditions of the poor. An interim report showed that the shortage of houses was acute, but still the Committee of Enquiry did not advocate a policy of municipal house building. The Committee recommended that estates should be purchased for development and that roads, sewers and other amenities should be prepared, but that private developers should build and sell/rent the houses. No less that 50,000 houses were required. There was a reluctance to spend public money, the capital expenditure for which would be enormous, but in any case the outbreak of war prevented the Committee from continuing its enquiries.

eight

Homes Fit for Heroes

In July 1917, while the war still raged, the Government issued an appeal to local authorities to plan house-building programmes. Private enterprise, it judged, would be unable to deal successfully or speedily with the backlog of house building, exacerbated by the war. It offered substantial financial assistance to local authorities if they were to instigate a programme of house building for the working classes. In 1918 the Housing and Town Planning Committee reported to the City Council. The estimated normal requirement of the city was 2,500 new houses per year, but owing to the lack of development over the previous decade, not helped by the war, 12,000 houses were now needed. This figure did not take into account extra housing requirements that would follow the intended slum housing clearance in the central area. The Ministry of Health reported that in Birmingham, with an estimated population of 910,000, there were 194,352 houses, of which 150,000 were working-class houses, many of which were not fit for habitation. It was estimated that 14,500 houses would be required within three years.

The Council was determined not to repeat the mistakes of the past. As a consequence they produced Town Planning Schemes to control the location and type of development. Features of these schemes included the determining of road widths, widening of old roads, provision of open spaces and housing density – usually twelve houses to the acre. The first two schemes were adopted in 1913. The Quinton, Harborne & Edgbaston Scheme was originally conceived in 1910. The East Birmingham Scheme proposed to deal in retrospect with the redevelopment of the established suburbs of Saltley, Washwood Heath, Ward End, Little Bromwich and Small Heath. In the post-war period, the first scheme covered north Yardley and Stechford. It was introduced in 1921. The South Birmingham Scheme, covering Acocks Green, Moseley, King's Heath, Yardley Wood and parts of King's Norton, was introduced in 1925. Schemes were also drafted for North Birmingham, Perry Barr in 1928, and Sheldon in 1931. Plans were also prepared for the other districts of the city. It was during this period that the concept of a green belt around the city was established. The Moundsley Hall Estate was purchased in 1937, with the specific intention of retaining it as an open space. Woodgate Valley was acquired as part of the South-west Birmingham Town Planning Scheme, and incorporated into the green belt. Other land followed as and when it came onto the market.

In May 1919 a contract was approved for the building of eighty-one houses in Linden Road, Bournville. It was small, but a start. In July, the Housing Committee bought up two estates at King's Heath, part of the estate of Mr G.W. Taylor. They were the 230-acre estate bounded by Wheelers Lane, Brook Lane, Yardley Wood Road and Haunch Lane, and the 79-acre estate bounded by Mill Pool Hill, the Stratford-upon-Avon Canal and Yardley Wood Road, including Cocks Moor Woods, some 42 acres set aside for open spaces under the South Birmingham Town Planning Scheme. These two estates, plus the previously purchased Pineapple and Fordhouse Farm Estates, were laid out for the development of 989 houses. Already underway were a number of smaller schemes. By Christmas 1919, Messers A.W. Wheater had built fifty houses in Cotterills Lane, Alum Rock, for the Council, at a cost of £800 per house. The firm of B. Whitehouse & Sons built twelve houses along Yardley Road, at a total cost of £10,560, and twenty-eight houses in Belchers Lane for £26,996. Under the Housing and Town Planning Act of 1919, the Council acquired on lease disused army huts at Castle Bromwich, and these were converted into dwellings for 106 families. That same December the Housing & Estates Committee, as it had become, accepted the offer from Henry Boot & Sons, a London firm of builders, to erect 1,000 houses on the Quinton Estate at a cost of £811 to £819 per house. There was a further proposal to build 500 houses in Washwood Heath, taking advantage of the nearby tram route.

In January 1920, as the Council proposed to acquire a 19½-acre site along the Chester Road, opposite Pype Hayes Park, for the building of 175 houses, a number of proposals were received from commercial builders to build houses for the Council. M.C.H. Hougham proposed to build fifty houses in Monica Road, Small Heath, at a cost of £5,550. There was an offer to develop an 18½-acre site at the junction of Marsh Lane and Reservoir Road, Stockland Green (suitable for 182 houses). Builders, F.J. Bull offered to build six houses in Tessall Lane, Northfield, at a cost of £850 per house, and on the Birchfield Estate 129 houses were offered by W.J. Phillips of Handsworth. H.M. Grant proposed to build fifty houses for the Council on a 5½-acre site at the junction of Station and Northfield Roads, King's Norton, and a further thirty-four houses at Abbey Road, Erdington, while Messers Dale & Waring proposed to build seventy-one houses at St Joseph's Road, Ward End.

In 1922 council-house building was taken over by the Public Works and Town Planning Committee. As they looked at the problem of clearing slum housing within the central area of the city, the difficulty of obtaining sufficient land and its prohibitive cost ruled out low-density replacement housing for those displaced whose occupations necessitated them to live within the central area. The only alternative was the construction of flats or maisonettes. Undeveloped land within the city centre was bought up. On a small uneven piece of land near the Birmingham City football ground, an experimental block of 180 flats was built in Garrison Lane in 1927-28 at a cost, including the land, of £96,429. Built in a distinctively Flemish style, the development was of fifteen blocks of three-storey buildings. On the old Cavalry Barracks site in Great Brook Street, the Ashcroft Estate was built, a development of 175 two-storey maisonettes. The scheme was intended to re-house those people displaced by the clearance of slums in the New Summer Street area near Summer Lane. In 1937, a second block of ninety-eight maisonettes was built at Kingston Hill, Coventry Road, on a site leased for 999 years from Birmingham University.

In March 1931, following a fact-finding trip to the Continent by the Estates and Public Works Committees, a recommendation was made to the City Council to erect a block of flats, to be officially known as St Martin's Flats, on a 5-acre site bounded by Angelina Street, Dymoke Street, Leopold Street and Vaughton Street. Emily Street bisected the area. While Council officials negotiated the purchase of the slum properties, tenders were invited. Messers G. Gray Wornum and A.C. Tripe were the winners. Their plans involved the building of 267 one-, two- and three-bedroom flats. Owing to the continuing shortage of skilled bricklayers, most of whom were working for private developers, it was decided to use concrete construction. The flats were four storeys in height, the floors of solid reinforced concrete. Every modern facility and amenity was included in the build. Each flat had a balcony. Refuse disposal chutes were placed opposite all staircases, and lifts were provided. The completed scheme had a central garden with seats and shelters. The first phase of the development was opened by Queen Elizabeth on 1 March 1939.

The extension of the city on 1 April 1928 with the annexation of Perry Barr provided the land necessary for the continuation of house building. Over £250,000 was spent on providing mains drainage prior to development. Three years later a portion of Castle Bromwich, Minworth, Solihull and Sheldon were brought into the city, and further land became available for house building. On 30 July 1930 the 30,000th municipal council house to be built was formally opened on the Kingstanding Estate by Arthur Greenwood, Minister for Health. Three years later, on 23 October, Neville Chamberlain, Chancellor of the Exchequer and former Lord Mayor of Birmingham, opened the 40,000th house at Weoley Castle. The completion of the 50,000th municipal house was celebrated on 20 June 1939 when the Lord Mayor, Ald. J. Crump, opened a four-bedroom house at Fellmeadow Road, Lea Hall Estate, Yardley.

In the inter-war period over 110,000 houses, council and private, were built in Birmingham, creating a suburban outer ring of houses far greater than the entire city as it existed in 1918. Almost 50 per cent of this housing stock was Council-built dwellings. It was a higher proportion of houses, streets and land utilization than any other city outside London. By 1939 council houses covered one eighth of the city's area, 5,380 acres, and 200,000 people had been rehoused. This was a fifth of the

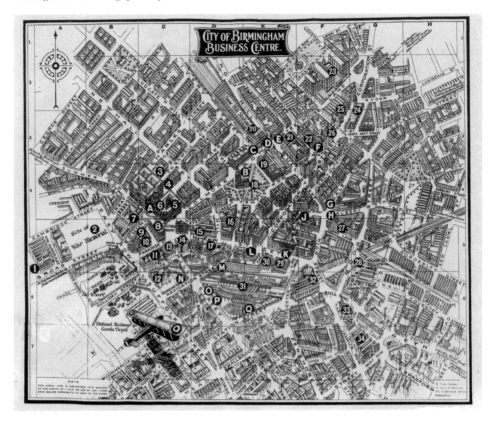

Birmingham, 1928. Self-confident and vibrant, the second city expanded beyond recognition in the inter-war period.

city's estimated population of 995,039. Sixty million bricks were used, and the cost of building 50,000 council houses was £23.5 million. The principal council estates developed in the inter-war years were:

Billesley Estates

The Billesley Estates comprise Billesley Farm, Billesley Common and Billesley House and May Lane Estates. They extend over an area of about 650 acres in King's Heath and Yardley Wood. The estates were developed over a period of years from 1919 to 1931. Some 3,500 council houses were erected here. In addition some houses were built on parts of Billesley Common by private developers. Provision was made for open spaces and recreation grounds, including Billesley Common Recreation Ground, and Trittiford Park. Bus services were established to serve the estates and, in addition, a train service was available from Yardley Wood Station.

Pype Hayes Estate

Situated on both sides of the purpose-cut Tyburn Road in Erdington, the estate is about 150 acres in size and lies between Chester Road and Kingsbury Road. The estate fronting Tyburn Road was brought into being by the Housing Act of 1919. The estate was developed between 1925 and 1929. Some 1,300 houses were built here. A large park was provided for the estate and land either side of a small stream running from Tyburn Road to Paget Road was established as an open space.

Marlborough House Estate

This 200-acre estate is situated at Yardley, about 4 miles from the city centre. It was developed between 1925 and 1930. Several of the original lanes in the area were widened to meet the needs of the new estate, and two arterial roads, Bordesley Green East and Hobmoor Road, were constructed. A 13½-acre site was established for recreational purposes, and the river valley of the Cole was laid out as parkland. Nearly 2,200 houses were eventually built on this estate.

Batchelors Farm Estate

An estate of almost 1,400 houses was built on a 100-acre site in Bordesley Green, bordered in the north by the former L.M.S. Railway line. It was developed between 1924 and 1927. A major 100 feet wide arterial road, Bordesley Green East, was constructed to serve the estate. Allotments were provided for leisure on both the eastern and the western sides of Batchelors Farm Estate. Parkland was also laid out on either side of the river Cole, which runs through the eastern part of the estate.

Fox Hollies & Gospel Farm Estates

These were built as adjoining estates covering nearly 400 acres and straddling the suburbs of Acocks Green and Hall Green, with over 3,700 houses, pushing right up to the city boundary with Solihull. Two major arterial roads, Olton Boulevard East and Fox Hollies Road, were cut to serve the estates, which were developed between 1926 and 1931. Open spaces were provided, including Fox Hollies Park, bordering onto Gospel Lane.

Tyseley Farm & Spring Road

This estate of three small adjoining sites, extending to 111 acres and consisting of over 1,300 houses, was built between 1927-28. The estate borders onto the Fox Hollies Estate, and is bisected by a section of Olton Boulevard.

Bushmore Farm Estate

Consisting of about 84 acres, this estate lies to the south of Gospel Farm Estate and was developed between 1930 and 1932. It is bounded by Gospel Lane, Lakey Lane and the city boundary with Solihull at Olton. Some 956 houses were built, as well as shops, situated at road junctions, and a large junior and infants school.

Allens Cross Estate

This is an estate built on the undulating land of the former Allens Cross Farm, situated to the west of the Bristol Road in Northfield. Not far from Frankley Reservoir,

The construction of the Kingstanding Estate, September 1929.

more that 2,100 houses were built here between 1929 and 1934. Shops were built, and two schools, Trescott and Bellfield Junior and Infants, were provided.

Tennal Hall & Tennal Lane Estates

Consisting of 90 acres, these two estates were developed piece-meal from 1929. Nearly 950 houses were built here. West Boulevard, a 120 feet wide arterial road, was cut through the estate, linking up the Hagley and Bristol Roads. Original lanes were widened where necessary, including Tennal Lane, widened to 100 feet, providing a major link to Harborne village. Just prior to the Second World War, the former golf course was laid out for development and the building of 342 houses was begun. The war intervened and plans to extend the estates to include Quinton and Ridgeacre Roads, with an additional 750 houses, were not completed.

Kingstanding & Kettlehouse Estates

These two adjoining estates, together covering approximately 700 acres, were begun in 1929, just after Perry Barr's incorporation into the city and over 6,300 houses were built. Some of the old roads were widened to double carriageways, and Kingstanding Circle, on the edge of the estate, was built as a civic centre with shops, a public house and a cinema. Playing fields and parkland, as well as an ancient wood and pre-historic mound, were provided or laid out for public use. The 300,000[th] house to be built for the Corporation is situated on the Kingstanding Estate, which borders onto Sutton Coldfield to the north-east, and the 137-acre Witton Lodge Estate of 1,374 houses, to the south.

Above: Hurlingham Road on the Kingstanding Estate, 1932.

Right: Kettlehouse Estate.

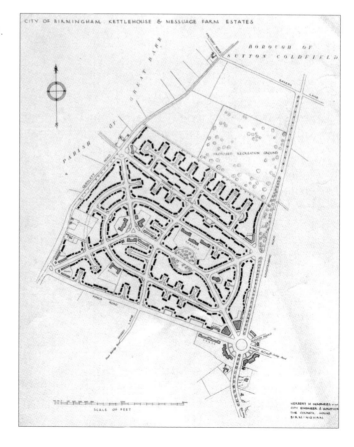

Aerial view of the Witton Lodge Estate. The geometric design was typical of 1930s council estates.

The cutting of Perry Common Road, July 1925.

Weoley Castle Estate

Four miles from the city centre, this estate takes its name from a thirteenth-century fortified manor house. Situated just beyond Selly Oak, off the Bristol Road, the estate covers an area of 312 acres. Developed between 1931 and 1934, the estate contains 2,178 houses. The land is gently undulating, and several small wooded areas were retained during the development, which was undoubtedly an influence from the nearby Bournville Estate. Wide grass verges were provided along the roads, and trees were planted. A large green was laid out at the centre of the estate, and shops, banks and other public buildings were built at this focal point. The 400,000[th] council house was opened here on 23 October 1933. Adjoining the Weoley Castle Estate to the north, on the other side of Stonehouse brook, is the Stonehouse Farm Estate. It covers an area of over 60 acres, and was developed between 1936-37, with over 600 houses.

Lea Hall Estate

Situated about 5 miles east of the city centre on a 450-acre site, development on this estate was begun in 1936. A railway line bisects the estate, which is served by Lea Hall Station. A 135-feet wide dual carriageway, Meadway, was also cut as part of a major arterial route linking the city via Bordesley Green East and Coleshill. Development of the estate, because of the railway, was undertaken as two entities. Nearly 3,500 houses were planned for the Lea Hall Estate, with parks and open spaces extending to 38 acres. An industrial area of some 40 acres was laid out on the north side of the railway line. In 1939 the 50,000[th] municipal house was opened here at 26, Fellmeadow Road.

Oscott College Estate

The 84-acre estate, about 4½ miles from the city centre, adjoins the Roman Catholic seminary of the same name. Developed in the late 1930s, it was laid out to accommodate 850 mixed, one- to five-bedroom dwellings, including twenty-four bungalows for older people.

Mill Pool Estate

Extending to the city boundary, this estate is bounded by the Alcester Road, Stratford-upon-Avon Canal and the Daisy Farm Estate. It is 169 acres in size and was purchased or leased over a period of years. Some 500 houses were initially built on the southern part of the estate, with further development in 1937. Building the 655 houses envisaged, including thirty-two bungalows for older people, was halted by the onset of war.

Kents Moat Estate

Adjoining Lea Hall Estate on its southern edge, Kents Moat Estate was developed from 1939 with the intention of building 1,200 dwellings, ranging from large five-bedroom family houses to bungalows for older people. Sheldon Heath Road was extended to serve the community. A sportsground off Sedgemere Road was provided, and the moat was laid out in its own grounds as a civic amenity.

Municipal Estates
Built in the Inter-War Years

Name of Estate	Situation	Area in Acres	No. of Houses Built or Provided
Kingstanding Perry Bar	North of city adjoining Sutton Coldfield	493	4,802
Kettlehouse Perry Barr	North side of Kingstanding Estate	204	1,500
Witton Lodge Farm Perry Barr	South side of Kingstanding Estate	137	1,374
Oscott College Perry Barr	South of Kingstanding Estate	84	859
Pype Hayes Erdington	North-east of the city/Chester and Kingsbury Roads	152½	1,344
Birches Green Erdington	Adjoining Pype Hayes Estate on Tyburn Road and Bromford Lane	73	910
Batchelors Farm and Norton Boys Home Bordesley Green	From city centre to eastern boundary	101½	1,360
Glebe Farm Estate Stechford	Frontage to Cole Hall and Church Lanes	125½	735
The Riddings Estate Stechford	Adjoining Glebe Farm Estate on west boundary	54½	600
Lea Hall Estate Stechford	Adjoining Glebe Farm Estate on east boundary	466½	3,486
Kent's Moat Stechford	Adjoining Lea Hall Estate	109	1,227
Marlborough House and Fast Pits Farm Yardley	South-east of Batchelors Farm Estate	200	2,171
Waterloo Farm and Stonehurst Estates South Yardley	Off Coventry Road at Waterloo Road	25¼	326
Haybarn Farm Small Heath	West of Marlborough House on Coventry Road	122	1,041
Tyseley Farm and Spring Road Acock's Green	South of Warwick Road Olton	111	1,350

Fox Hollies and Gospel Farm Estates Acock's Green/Hall Green	Adjoining city south-east boundary between Warwick and Stratford Roads	393	3,762
Bushmore Farm Billesley Estates Yardley Wood	Adjoining south side of Gospel Farm and south and boundary of city	84	956
Ivyhouse Farm Yardley Wood	Frontages to Brook Lane and Yardley Wood Road	23½	312
Billesley Farm Estate	Frontages to Yardley Wood Road and Priory Road	3742	442
Billesley Common Estate	Frontage to Yardley Wood Road and Brook Lane, etc	230	127
Billesley House and May Lane Estates	Frontages to Yardley Wood Road, etc	43½	536
Daisy Farm Yardley Wood	Near Billesley Estates	73	712
Mill Pool Hill Yardley Wood	South side of the city adjoining Billesley Estates	169	655
Dads Lane, Shutlock Lane and Cartland Road, King's Heath	East of the Pershore Road at Ten Acres, adjoining Uffculme Park	114	1,114
Allen's Cross Farm, Northfield	Adjoining south-west boundary of city, off Bristol Rd, to Frankley Reservoir	194	2,161
Broadmeadow, King's Norton	Off Broadmeadow Lane and Parsons Hill	35	319
Weoley Castle, Nr Selly Oak	Off Bristol Road, 4 miles from city	312	2,718
Tennal Lane Extension, Quinton	Adjoining south boundary of Tennal Hall Estate, 4 miles from city centre	42½	525
Tennal Hall Estate, Quinton	Adjoining Quinton Lane and Tennal Lane	44¼	366
Quinton Estates, Quinton	West side of city adjoining Tennal Hall	76½	848
Stonehouse Farm, California	Adjoining north boundary of Weoley Castle Estate	63	604

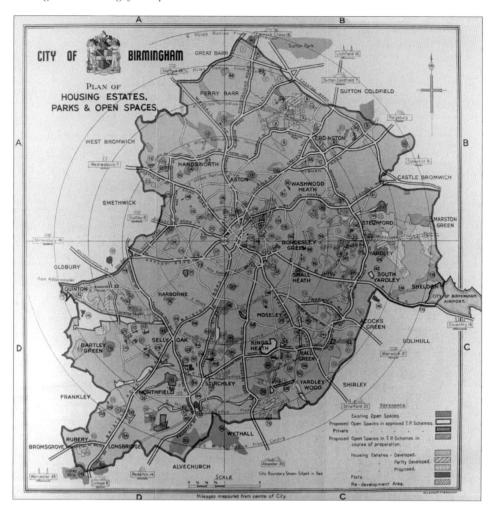

Birmingham council estates, 1939.

An inevitable consequence of building these badly needed estates in the semi-rural outer suburbs was that people inhabiting them were also moving away from their place of work. With some of the later estates, industrial areas were zoned next to them, but for the earlier estates it became necessary to transport large numbers of people from the outer, to the inner suburbs, each day. The way the Council solved this problem was to establish two circular bus services. The Inner Circle, No. 8, joined the inner suburbs in an 11-mile loop. It was introduced in 1928. The Outer Circle, No. 11, which proved to be one of the longest bus routes in the country, 25 miles in circuit, linked the outer suburbs. Special reduced workmen's fares were introduced. At the weekend sightseers used the route as a half-day tour of the city. With its many stops, the latter journey took just over two hours.

Perhaps the most common criticism of the new council estates referred to their blandness. The newspapers of the day speak of them as being soulless and monotonous. All the houses looked the same, it was claimed, and though this was not true on some estates, the perception was there. The estates were built in complex geometric patterns of straight lines intermixed with circles and crescents – shapes of the engineer rather than the architect. Private estates had gentle curves, and made better use of undulating land and existing trees and foliage. In the late 1930s this did change, as more land became available. Better use was made of natural features, and trees were planted as a matter of course. Houses became more varied, and building lines were broken up by constructing houses in blocks, and by setting them further back from the road.

In the inter-war period private developers built 56,191 houses in the suburbs between 1919 and 1939. By 1934 they had built 15,860 houses, but by the following year this had leapt up to an extraordinary 32,000 houses. Thereafter private developers built between 6,200 and 7,800 houses per year. Early stimulus for private house building was offered in the Housing (Additional Powers) Act of 1919. The Act made provision for financial assistance by the Government to builders for the erection of houses, subject to certification of satisfactory fitness by the local authority. Other Acts with similar enticements followed. In 1923 the Corporation, taking advantage of the powers of the Housing Act of that year, decided to encourage the erection of houses by private enterprise by passing on in a lump sum the Government subsidy of £6 per year, for twenty years. This was fixed at £100.

In 1924, Birmingham Mutual Housings Ltd took advantage of this offer and acquired 104.77 acres of land from Birmingham Corporation. The land was situated south of Moseley, and lay between Wheelers Lane, Haunch Lane and Yardley Wood Road. The new venture was called Holly Bank Village. The proposal was to build between 500 and 600 houses, designed by the architectural firm of Collier & Keyte, at a ratio of six houses to the acre, as well as thirty shops, a post office, a doctor's surgery, and a dentist. Homes were primarily semi-detached, with a garage, on a frontage of 11 to 12 yards. The cheapest houses cost between £650 and £700, while the more expensive cost between £850 and £1,000. All house owners held the freehold, with leases granted for ninety-nine years. The scheme received the full backing of the City Council. Within the estate the company proposed to lay out an 18-acre park, containing tennis courts and bowling greens. The Lord Mayor, Ald. Percival Bower, turned the first sod of this model village. In attendance was the Minister for Health, Birmingham MP Neville Chamberlain, and the MP for Moseley, P.J. Hannon.

The mid- to late 1930s period was the hey-day of the private developer. The former private estates at Yardley and Hall Green, after being laid out, were made available for development. Perry Barr, annexed in 1928, and later Sheldon, provided additional much-needed development land. The Severne Estate in Hall Green, originally sold off in 1912, was developed over a six-year period by Harry Dare & Son. They built 450 houses, a parade of twelve shops, an almshouse and a public house, The Three Magpies. The Severne Estate is made up of Lakey Lane, Shirley Road, School Road, Lulworth Road, Studland Road, Endsleigh Grove and Miall Road.

Part of the estate, comprising School Road and Miall Road, off Fox Hollies Road, was made a conservation area in 1988. Also during the 1930s Dare's developed the Little Derbyshire Estate off Robin Hood Lane, consisting of Kedleston Road, Etwall Road, Doveridge Road, Egginton and Dalbury Roads. They were later to go on to develop a number of other schemes, including an estate at Hodge Hill.

Middle-class Hall Green was one of the most favoured districts in Birmingham for private developers. The Mayfields Estate, developed in 1937-38, was built by the firms of. F. Spencer and Broomhead & Green, to the designs of architects Hewitt & Meredith. The estate was situated at the junction of Baldwins Lane and Barton Lodge Road. Houses ranged in price from £379 in Geoffrey Road, to £385 in Watwood Road, to £445 in Acheson Road, and up to £485 in Delrene Road. Unlike Council developments, which stopped at the border, the Mayfield Estate continued on into Shirley, which is part of Solihull. The same combination of firms designed and built the Hillside Estate in Sheldon, just off the Coventry Road, on the border of Birmingham and Olton, Solihull. In addition two other private estates were built at Sheldon, the Elms Park Estate and the New Sheldon Estate. To the left-hand side of Church Road, almost opposite Sheldon parish church, Messers A. Glover built the Elms Park Estate in 1937. Houses varied in price from £345 to £395. Messers E.L. Robinson and Messers J.C. Freeman & Son Ltd, built the New Sheldon Estate near the old village; a series of semi-detached houses and bungalows, with garage space, consisting of Elmay Road, Horrell Road, Larne Road, Benedon Road, Willcare Road, Hernall Croft and Kennedy Croft. Prices ranged from £375 to £500, according to size and specification. The added attraction for these two estates was the large open space nearby, presented to the King George V Jubilee Trust and laid out as playing fields.

Further down the Coventry Road at Lyndon Green, Stubbs Brothers developed the Gilbertstone Estate. It was a great swathe of land bounded by Manor House Lane, Barrows Lane and the Coventry Road. The firm built 1,373 houses, and created Heronsdale Road, Saxondale Road, Wensley Road, Wychwood Crescent, Westcombe Grove, Beachmore Road and Leavesden Grove, also building along the widened Brays Road. House prices varied from £380 to £585. Situated just to the north of Garrett's Green Lane, bounded by Cockshut Hill and the Municipal Sports Ground, is the Crofts Estate, built at the same time, and consisting of Bilton Grange Road, Charlbury Crescent, Welford Avenue, Gleneagles Road, Duncroft Road, Stancroft Grove, Stanton Grove and Ashdale Grove. House prices ranged from £359 to £495, and the selling agents were Jones, Mackay & Croxford of Edmund Street, Birmingham.

The Brandwood Park Estate, formerly Brandwood Golf Course, with commanding views over the countryside towards the Clent Hills, was laid out for development in 1937. Two companies, Birmingham Housing Industries and The Model Building Company of Black Heath, developed it to designs by the architectectural firms of L.E. Hewitt & Meredith, and Nicklin & Bull. The building work was undertaken by J.C. Freeman & Son Ltd, Messers F. Spencer of Erdington and A. Walker & Son

Private development in Sheldon.

The Gilbertstone Estate.

of Coleshill. The estate roads consisted of the southern side of Dawberry Fields Road, Brandwood Park Road, Yarningdale Road, Doversley Road, Valbourne Road, Kernthorpe Road, Bryndale Avenue, Shalnecote Drive, Denford Grove and Dulvern Grove. Houses varied in price from £425 to £615, while larger detached and semi-detached, matching quality, ranged from £675 to £799.

Also in King's Heath, further down the Alcester Road, about half a mile beyond Alcester Lanes End yet just within the city boundary, was built the Millpool Hill Farm Estate. It was a small estate, consisting of Marsham Road, Meadowfoot Avenue and Camford Grove. The houses, varying in price from £399 to £465, were built by two companies, Messers Matthews & Baker and L.& F. Baker. Houses were built on a ninety-nine-year lease, with ground rent of £5 10s per annum. The cheaper houses had two bedrooms and a box room, the more expensive, three bedrooms. Two bus services, Nos 35 and 17 were laid on to serve this little estate.

At Northfield, as the car trade expanded to new levels, Erdington builders Broomhead & Green built modest semis upon the Greenlands Estate. Conveniently situated adjoining the Austin works, these houses in Longbridge Lane were designed by architects A.J. White and Styles. With prices ranging from £355 to £375, with a down payment of £20 and weekly repayments of 14s 6½d a week, sale of these houses was aimed at car workers. Broomhead & Green were also responsible for the development of the Rock Farm Estate in Handsworth Wood. The estate is situated a short distance along Rocky Lane, not far from Great Barr Station. The firm, under the direction of the Birmingham and District House Builders Association, built a series of terraces of four houses, with a central entry, and roughcast on the upper storey. This house style, minus the roughcast, was also utilised on their Douglas Estate, off the Kingstanding Road at Dyas Avenue. The estate included Birdbrook Road, Harleston Road and Goodway Road. The advertising appeal was that the houses here were 'designed to give the greatest possible accommodation at a low price, and … appealing particularly to those who have to make the most of their weekly income'. The central three-bedroom houses sold for £355. The end houses, with two bedrooms, sold for £340. Ground rents were £5 10s per year. The Whyte & Styles/Broomhead & Green partnership also built the Berwood House Estate off Orphanage Road, between Erdington and Sutton Coldfield. A series of semi-detached houses with roughcast bay windows opposite Harman Road, were offered for sale with a garage (£585) or without (£545).

At Handsworth Wood, just off World's End Road, was another private development, the Cherry Orchard Estate. Accommodation here, with a sales price of £535 a house, was described as 'Superior fully-detached residences'. The estate is pleasantly situated with Perry Hall Playing Fields to one side and Handsworth Golf Course and Sandwell Park to the other. Not too far away, semi-detached houses with garage space and long garden plots were built in Beauchamp Avenue, off Hamstead Hill, by Messers Bull & Tewkesbury in 1937, at a cost of £460. Builders Bull & Tewkesbury, in partnership with architects Nicklin & Bull, were responsible for a number of inter-war estates. Half a mile beyond King's Norton village, between the Redditch and Rednal Roads, they constructed the Grange Farm Estate. Based on Aversley and Calverley Roads, they built a series of detached and semi-detached houses, rising in price to £575 for their 'Rutland' design detached house with garage. The Rutland design was repeated by the firm in a small development in Osmaston Road, Harborne, in 1938. On the Tinkers Farm Estate in Quinton, a short walk down Lewis Road, this design was used again along with others, the 'Surrey' and the 'Lincoln' designs. The Surrey was described as 'an ideal small house', a pleasing cottage-style semi with echoes of Harvey's Bournville Estate housing of tiles and upper gable windows. Prices at Tinkers Farm were more modest constructions, ranging from £410 to £510. The firm again used architects Nicklin & Bull who developed the Hollyfields Estate in Erdington. It consisted of developments along Holly Lane, Hollydale Road, Woodacre Road, Westmead Crescent, Welland and Turfton Groves, Springthorne, Varley and Pype Hayes Roads. Several designs were used in the construction, including in one case a nod to the German, Bauhaus.

Of all Birmingham's suburbs, Perry Barr, annexed in 1928, saw the greatest development during the inter-war years. Within a decade Perry Barr was changed from rural to urban. In addition to those estates already mentioned, Greenholm,

Above left: Bull & Tewkesbury built several estates in southern Birmingham.

Above right: The greatest development, both municipal and private, in the inter-war years was at Perry Barr.

Perry Hall and the Booth's Farm Estate were also developed. Overlooking playing fields, the Greenholm Estate situated in Greenholm Road, formerly Green Lane, Elmbridge, Anstey and Blakeland Roads, to the left-hand side of the Kingstanding Road, was developed by Taylor Woodrow Estates Ltd and offered a choice of four alternative designs, including a sort of Anglicised Bauhaus, with a space at the side for a garage. There was a further choice of two- or three-bedroom houses at £395 or £440.

The Perry Hall Estate, 3 miles from the city centre, is situated off the main Walsall Road. It contains two prominent tree-lined avenues, formerly leading to Perry Hall, the sixteenth-century home of the Roman Catholic Stanford family, and latterly the Gough family, who largely rebuilt the house in Victorian times. The house was later unfortunately demolished because it was considered at the time too expensive to maintain. The estate was developed during the 1930s by a number of builders, including Broomhead & Green and T. Warren Tew & Co. The estate was laid out in building plots, and several new roads off the Walsall Road were cut, including Glendower Road, Teddington Grove, Sandringham Road, Wensleydale Road, Lymedene Road, Cliveden Avenue, Derrydown Road, Pendragon Road, Wilnecote Grove, Ivybridge Grove and Carmodale Avenue, with further development along Rocky Lane and the entrance drive to the hall, Perry Avenue. A major selling point for the estate was its two neighbouring parks, Perry Hall Playing Fields and Perry Park, with Great Barr Park and Sutton Park a short bus ride away. It was also very well served by public transport. The No. 6 tram ran as far as Perry Barr Station, while bus Nos 29 and 29a served the Kingstanding Road and the Nos 118 and 189 Midland Red buses maintained a frequent service along the Walsall Road. Equally important was the new Outer Circle No. 11 bus route, linking Perry Barr with the industrial centres of Aston, Witton, Hockley and Lozells. House prices varied from two-bedroom houses at £360 in Carmodale Avenue, up to large, three-bedroom houses in Cliveden Avenue at £550. A little further along the Walsall Road was the Booths Farm Estate. Almost opposite Tower Hill, it was developed at the same time with a mixture of detached and semi-detached houses. Detached sold for between £400 and £430, while semis went for between £375 and £395. On the other side of the Walsall Road, the Tower Hill Estate, a continuation of the Perry Hall Estate, was developed from 1934 by Messers Handsworth Wood Estates Ltd, bringing into existence Yately Avenue, Yateley Crescent, Valley Crescent, Stanford Avenue, Charnwood Road, Rockford Road and Dyas Avenue. They built a number of estates in the district around the Great Barr area, just beyond the Birmingham border, incorporating housing designs by architectural firms including Batemans, Arthur McKewan, Cecil Fillmore, A.J. White & Styles, E.G. Harrison & Tracey and Skelcher, Machin & Watson.

Other estates developed by private builders include the Highfield Estate at Washwood Heath, situated within a short distance of, and designed to house, Wolseley motor works employees, the Hobs Farm Estate at Castle Bromwich, and the Whateley Hall Estate along the Chester Road, some 50 yards or thereabouts from the Bradford Arms. The Springfield Estate on the border of Hall Green and Moseley, a short distance from J.R.R. Tolkien's boyhood home, sold off in 1920, was developed during the 1930s, as was the Moor Hall Estate, Sutton. Also at Sutton Coldfield in 1933, Somerville Estate was allowed to build a row of twelve detached houses on Monmouth Drive. Permission being given by the then existing Sutton Borough Council on condition that the estate handed over a tract of land stretching from west of Powell Pool and along the Drive into Clifton Road, incorporating Windley Pool almost as far as Park Road, which was incorporated into Sutton Park. Finally there was the Weoley Park Farm Estate, Gibbins Road, Selly Oak. Situated just off the Bristol Road, and approached from Harborne Lane via Gibbins Road. New roads brought into being included Durley Dean Road, Corisande Road, Woolacombe Lodge Road, Strathdene Road, Widney Avenue and Falconhurst Road. There was little variation in price, £385 to £399, depending on the inclusion or non-inclusion of electric fires in the two main bedrooms.

In addition to the large estates there were a number of small developments, mainly infill of land left over after the Council and private developers had built their estates. These plots were picked up by the smaller building firms in the city as speculative ventures. Usually they consisted of anything from one up to maybe half a dozen semi-detached houses. Apart from houses, provision was also made in these new suburban developments for schools, community halls and other civic amenities including cinemas and public houses. The 1930s was the great age of the cinema, vividly portrayed by Oscar Deutsch's Art Deco-designed Odeon cinemas chain. There are two very good surviving examples, and it is hard to choose between them – the Kingstanding Odeon and the Sutton Odeon. 'Odeon' it was light-heartedly said, stood for 'Oscar Deutsch Entertains Our Nation'. In addition to the numerous cinemas that originated in the inter-war period, this was also the age of the large brewers' pubs, built in the outer suburbs, epitomised best of all by the Black Horse at Northfield. It was designed by Francis Goldborough of Bateman & Bateman for Davenports, and opened in 1929. Thankfully this building is now protected by a Grade II-listing, but sadly the equally splendid Kingstanding, built in the style of a red-brick Tudor mansion, and with the longest bar in Birmingham, was demolished in the late 1960s.

In the centre of Birmingham redevelopment began once more in an area designated the Civic Centre. In October 1919 the Council acquired, at a cost of £100,000, a large site bounded by Broad Street, Easy Row, Cambridge Street and Baskerville Place. In July 1922 work began on clearing the site. The first building erected here was the Hall of Memory, a war memorial to honour the city's 12,920 sons who fell in the First World War. The builders were John Barnsley & Son. This octagonal building, in the Roman Doric style, was opened in 1925. The following year work began on the clearance of further land for the building of Municipal offices. Due to the Depression, it was not until 1937 that the Council gave its authority to proceed. T. Cecil Howitt was chosen as the architect. The Lord Mayor, Cllr E.R. Canning, laid the foundation stone on 27 June 1938. By July 1939 the east wing of the Civic Centre was complete. The war and post-war recession halted any further development of the site. In March 1961 the building was renamed Baskerville House. Across the road, the Municipal Bank, brainchild of former Lord Mayor Neville Chamberlain, was opened on 27 November 1933 by Prince George, later Duke of Kent. It too was designed by T. Cecil Howitt. His building, in the Ionic Neo-Classical style, reflects the general classic design of the proposed Civic Centre. By the end of the 1930s another world war was looming and with many a former hero still living in 'conditions unfit for human habitation', improvements and building development once again came to a halt.

nine

The Post-War Decade

At eleven minutes after one o'clock on the night of 9 August 1940, a lone bomber, presumably looking for Fort Dunlop or the Nuffield Shadow Aero factory, missed his target and dropped a clutch of bombs on a suburban street in Erdington. One man was killed and six people were wounded. There had been no prior air-raid warning. The all clear was sounded just after 2.30 a.m. This attack was followed over the next three weeks by a series of small raids, mostly concentrating on the industrialised east side of the city. On the night of 25/26 August the bombers changed their tactics and raided the city centre. They destroyed the Market Hall and other premises nearby, causing twenty-five civilian casualties. Other night-time attacks followed, but the Luftwaffe failed to conciliate the damage they caused. They did not bomb on consecutive nights, thus allowing the defenders to reorganise. The effect of consecutive bombing could have been disastrous, creating a fire-storm. After the raid of 22 November 1940, water supplies were cut off for five days, but thankfully no further raids came on the following nights. Between 9 August 1940 and the last raid on 23 April 1943, Birmingham suffered a total of seventy-seven air raids. Sutton Coldfield was bombed twice, apparently unintentionally. Some 2,128 civilians were killed in Birmingham, and over 3,000 seriously injured; 12,000 houses were damaged, 4,000 of them beyond repair, and over 1,000 factories, offices, shops and public buildings were destroyed.

In 1942 Cllr Norman Tiptaft became Lord Mayor and founded a new committee, the Reconstruction Committee, whose function was to co-ordinate the work of all the other committees planning for peacetime. Unlike the First World War, which began as a summer campaign and dragged on for four years, the Second World War was anticipated as a long struggle and planning ahead was possible and done. The three main recommendations of the Birmingham committees involving physical reconstruction to be considered were:

The Blitz on Birmingham paved the way for the 1960s redevelopment of the city centre.

Those slums not destroyed by the Blitz were cleared away from the 1950s onwards.

a. The building of more houses; 100,000 in fifteen years. b. Slum clearance, taking advantage of the bombings. c. Better roads and in particular the construction of an inner ring road.

With the arrival of peace, Birmingham already had a coherent housing policy, with five defined redevelopment areas. These were areas whose buildings and the layout of its roads had become obsolescent. They were districts that had outlived the conditions of life for which they were designed, and provided a living and working environment far below acceptable contemporary standards. In February 1946 the Council made the Compulsory Purchase Order that was needed to buy up some 30,000 sub-standard dwellings, in order to demolish them, clear the sites and build new houses. Added finance came in the wake of the Labour Government's Housing Act of 1946, providing subsidies to local authorities to fulfil its promise of building 240,000 new houses nationwide per year. There was a national shortage though of skilled labour and building materials, and as a consequence priority was often given to industrial reconstruction; the country was near bankrupt, and in debt to the USA. It was not until the summer of 1948 that work began on the demolition of slum property, meanwhile, slowly at first, building work was continued at Kitts Green, Sheldon, Shard End, Tile Cross and Lea Hall to house those displaced by slum clearance in central Birmingham. Private development continued in the outer

House Building in Birmingham
(1945-1955)

Year	Corporation	Private Developers
1945	6	25
1946	413	550
1947	826	667
1948	1,400	470
1949	1,227	470
1950	2,016	671
1951	3,467	555
1952	4,744	765
1953	4,006	781
1954	3,005	918
1955	3,010	848

suburbs and on small pockets of land in the inner city. A typical example of such a build was the Links Estate at King's Norton, developed in 1946. Here Selly Oak builder Bertram S. White, of Frederick Road, erected a small estate of twenty-five houses along newly created Grassmoor Road, Fairmead Rise and Hazelbank. Prices on the 12½-acre development ranged between £750 and £900 per house, depending upon location. It was the continuation of a pre-war development by White, the original conveyance of which permitted a development of 125 houses. At the Whateley Hall Estate, Castle Bromwich, Hales & Co. built 116 semi-detached houses, thirty of which they rented out at £2 0s 6d per week, without rates. By the end of the first decade, private builders were erecting almost one third of all houses being built in the city.

Across the border in Sutton Coldfield, the Royal Borough had to deal with an increase in population caused by a number of factors, including Brummies who had fled from the Blitz-threatened city to this relatively safe suburb. In the summer of 1946, a piece of land fronting Springfield Road, having an area of 4.6 acres and owned by Sutton Coldfield Trustees of Municipal Charities, was purchased for £1,150, with a view to building a 198-acre municipal housing estate to be known as Falcon Lodge. In addition, the Council sought to acquire smaller plots in and around the town centre. One of these was a tract of land on the corner of Lindridge Road and Rectory Road. That July the borough surveyor entered into a contract with local builder Mr F.A. Carpenter for his firm to erect twenty-two houses in Coppice

Construction of Houses in Sutton Coldfield*
(1945-1951)

Site	Area in acres	No. of houses erected	No. of houses to be erected
1. Blackberry Lane (west side)	5.8	44	44
2. Blackberry Lane (eastside)	3	31	36
3. Tower Road	35	226	264
4. Cottage Lane, Minworth	6.5	--	50
5. Falcon Lodge	198	--	1,500
6. Coppice View, off Chester Road	2.5	14	22
7. Maxstoke Road (Old peoples' bungalows)	1.5	12	12
8. Tower Road. (Old peoples' bungalows)	5	6	6
9. Windyridge Road (Cat Hill Estate)	6.84	72	72
10. Clarence Road			

Total permanent houses — 405 — 2006

In addition 100 pre-fabs were erected in various parts of the Borough

Permanent houses erected between 1919 and 1939 — 609

* As at 30th June 1951

119

The post-war redevelopment of Dudeston and Nechells.

View Road, just off the Chester Road. The Corporation agreed to purchase them for £23,197 18s 0d, plus £2,956 10s 0d, being the cost of the land. On 9 September 1946, the keys of the first four houses of twelve in Blackberry Lane, the first of Sutton's post-war council houses, were handed over to their new tenants.

Plans for the Falcon Lodge Estate were drawn up and approved, and the South Staffordshire Water Works Company laid a 12-inch main to serve the new estate. Unfortunately the Ministry of Works now stepped in, following consideration being given to a national House Building Programme, and requested the Council not to proceed with the development. Following clarification, in November 1947 the Council advertised for tenders to be submitted for the initial erection of twenty-eight houses fronting Springfield Road. The first house on the proposed 1,500-dwelling estate was opened by the Lord Mayor C.H. Dainty, in January 1949. Shortage of building materials after the war caused delays, and it was not until the early 1960s that the estate was finally completed.

With the construction of new housing well underway, the demolition of slum properties in Birmingham began. In 1950 clearance began in the Great Francis Street area of Nechells. By 1953 work was in progress on all five of the redevelopment areas. The first of four twelve-storey blocks of flats, Queen's Tower, at the junction of Great Francis Street and Great Lister Street, was opened in 1954 by the Conservative

Minister for housing, and later by Prime Minister Harold Macmillan. Work also began in the Ladywood Redevelopment Area (Units 202–203), just off Broad Street near Five Ways. Here eighty-four, three-storey flats and forty-eight houses were built, on reclaimed land. In the Ledsam Street area (Unit 205), almost 10 acres of land, on which 400 substandard houses stood, 311 dwellings were erected. These were a mixture of four- and six-storey maisonettes, and one eleven-storey block containing forty-four flats. It was high-density build, but given the scarcity and high price of land just beyond the town centre, it was the only economic way to build. Despite this, an 8½-acre cleared site in Bell Barn Road was set aside as a park and children's playground for the tenants of what was to become the Lee Bank Estate.

In a bid to reduce its waiting list for new houses, the Council acquired the 186-acre Kingshurst Hall Estate across the border at Coleshill in Warwickshire in 1952. After negotiating with Meriden Rural Council, they were permitted to build 2,000

Building the new houses and flats, Nechells, *c.* 1956.

houses, and agreed to provide council housing for people on Meriden's housing list. The mixed development of the new estate provided homes for 7,000 people, at an estimated cost of £3 million. Two thirds of the municipal development went to Dare & Sons Ltd. Interestingly the development allowed for a mixture of municipal and private houses, in the ratio of 80% and 20% respectively. Private development was undertaken at the Bacon's End side of the estate, where 300 houses were constructed near the Chester Road. By December 1952, with a number of estates under construction or seeking approval, it was calculated by council officers that there was only enough remaining private land in Birmingham to build 6,000 houses. Other cross-border developments had to follow, with schemes agreed with Droitwich, Tamworth, Redditch and Daventry.

In December 1952, Alderman Bradbeer, Chairman of the House Building Committee, announced the purchase of the 14-acre Valley Farm Estate near Beacon Hill, Rednal, with a view to letting it for private development. At the same meeting Bradbeer also announced the authorisation for the development of 216 multistorey flats on a site at Aston Reservoir near Salford Recreation Ground. Four twelve-storey blocks, each 110 feet high, and three four-storey blocks were proposed. By the first week of 1953 the Council had built 20,000 houses since work had resumed on 1 April 1945. Three new estates were given approval for development: Each Way Farm and Leach Green Estates at Rubery, and Holifast Grange at Erdington. Meanwhile the development of Bartley Green continued on the 200-acre Corporation Estate, 650 feet above sea level, bounded by Adams Hill, Kitwell Lane, Wood Lane and Scotland Lane. Approval was also given to the development of two further estates, Rubery Farm and Dowry Farm, Rubery, and the Firs Estate at Castle Bromwich, next to the Hodge Hill Estate. Situated on sloping ground near Rubery Hospital, the Rubery Estate was designed to house 2,022 people in a mixture of 487 dwellings, varying from single-bedroom bungalows to Y-shaped, six storey blocks of flats. The Firs, situated close to the river Tame, was designed to accommodate 4,000 people in 1,096 mixed dwellings, varying from one- to four-bedroom houses, bungalows and multi-storey flats. The layout gave a density of eighteen dwellings to the acre, much higher than usual, indicating the pressure upon a scarce resource. The estate was difficult to develop owing to drainage difficulties and the steep contours on part of the estate. At Hawkesley six-storey flats in loaded brickwork were approved – the first time the Corporation had agreed to build flats over three storeys without steel. By Christmas 1952, construction had just begun on two new adjoining estates between King's Norton and Northfield. The Bunbury Road development consisted of 500 dwellings, connected by Pope's Lane to the Wychall Farm Estate, also of 500 dwellings. Here the emphasis was on two-, three- and six-storey blocks of flats. The building of the Bunbury Road Estate saw a radical departure in development policy. Preparatory work, the laying of sewers, drains and the cutting of roads, as well as the building of the houses and flats, were carried out by a private firm, John Laing & Son Ltd. The shells of the houses, constructed in poured concrete, could be put up, from foundations to roof level, in just eight days.

In the autumn of 1953 work was begun on a new 500-dwelling housing estate at Ley Hill, completing the link between two pre-war estates, Weoley Castle and Allens Cross. Overlooking Frankley Beeches, bequeathed to the city as parkland by George Cadbury, when built, the estate at Ley Hill also linked up with a recently built estate at Bangham Pit. A shopping centre was developed at Merritts Hill to serve the two communities.

As land in the outer suburbs became scarce, Council officials looked at brown field sites in the inner city. The legacy of the late war – bombed sites – offered opportunities for minor building schemes. In February 1953 the Council began negotiations for the acquisition of bombed sites around Havelock Road, Saltley, with the intention of building sixty houses. Further land at the junction of the Coventry Road at its junction with Bordesley Park Road was also acquired. It was a small plot, upon which eight one-bedroom flats were built. It was a measure of the desperation felt, in a city where 100,000 newcomers had settled since the end of the war.

Work continued on other developments. On the Stapenhall Farm Estate, between Northfield and West Heath, the Council entered into negotiations with Wates Ltd, the London firm of builders and civil engineers. In a £516,000 deal signed in May 1954, the firm agreed to build 268 dwellings in the form of six six-storey blocks of flats and five four-storey blocks of maisonettes, constructed in brick and reinforced concrete. In July 1954, city architect A.G. Sheppard Fidler revealed his plans to develop a cleared slum area in Ladywood. The new estate, lying between Great Tindal Street, Browning Street, Morville Street and Ledsam Street, was designed so that residents would look inwards onto quiet squares and grassed courts. It was high-density development of 311 dwellings rising from three-storey maisonettes to eleven-storey blocks of flats. Pressure mounted in the Redevelopment Areas when it became impossible to re-house some 49,000 of the displaced population. It became necessary to move them to other estates, or even across the city boundary. As pressure mounted, desired density went by the board, and higher and higher blocks of flats were built. At Newtown there were eventually blocks of up to twenty storeys, and at Lee Bank, the Sentinels, either side of Holloway Head, were thirty-two storeys high. The Corporation, desperately short of land for building, managed to secure 48 acres, in dribs and drabs, from Birmingham Regional Hospital Board. Around Rubery, it consisted of 2.75 acres of land at Rubery Hill and Hollymoor Mental Hospitals, in a small triangular detached plot to the north of Hollymoor. At Monyhull Hospital they acquired approximately 40 acres, mainly along the eastern and southern boundaries of the hospital estate, and at Agatha Stacey Mental Deficiency Hostel at Rednal, just over 5 acres.

As Lady Megan Lloyd George planted a tree on the Kingshurst Estate on 4 February 1955 to celebrate the opening of the city's 21,000[th] post-war dwelling, Housing chairman, Ald. A.F. Bradbeer, spoke of providing accommodation for 100,000 people beyond Birmingham's boundary. Birmingham, he revealed, needed about 7,500 acres in the adjoining counties of Worcestershire, Staffordshire and Warwickshire. Sutton Coldfield's response was swift. 'I very much doubt whether

The Lee Bank development.

there would be any land available in Sutton Coldfield', Town Planning Chairman, Cllr A.G. Hilton responded. 'It is becoming difficult to find plots for very small groups of houses in the borough.' Solihull however was more accommodating. Following talks in December 1955 between the two authorities, a joint statement issued stated: 'Members of both corporations had a friendly, full, free and frank discussion on the problems of overspill, and representatives will be reporting back to their own authorities on the matter'. Officials at Dawley in Shropshire were more positive. They agreed to take 10,000 of Birmingham's overspill, and put forward a proposal to build a satellite town to house 100,000 people. The town, Dawley New Town, was later renamed Telford.

Within Birmingham itself, the Corporation successfully negotiated the purchase of 100 acres from the Calthorpe Estate in May 1955. The four large areas of land were built up with villa-type houses with large gardens. They were:

Area A: nearly 10 acres, bounded by Belgrave Road, Pershore Road, Balsall Heath Road and Bristol Road.

Area B: nearly 17 acres, bounded by Balsall Heath Road, Pershore Road, Speedwell Road and Bristol Road.

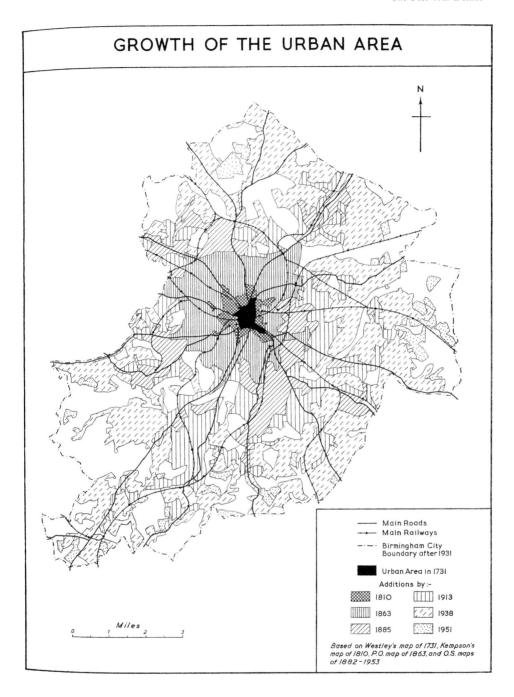

GROWTH OF THE URBAN AREA

N

Main Roads
Main Railways
Birmingham City
Boundary after 1931

Urban Area in 1731

Additions by :-

1810   1913
1863   1938
1885   1951

Based on Westley's map of 1731, Kempson's map of 1810, P.O. map of 1863, and O.S. maps of 1882-1953

Miles
0   1   2   3

The growth of Birmingham up to 1953.

Area C: 50 acres, bounded by Belgrave Road, the river Rea, Speedwell Road and Pershore Road.

Area D: 24½ acres, bounded by Monument Road, Plough & Harrow Road, Beaufort Road, Duchess Road, Francis Road and Ladywood Road.

Three years later the Calthorpe Estate issued its own Master Plan. The plan was prepared by Birmingham architect John Madin, who later went on to design the Central Library. H.E. Greening, agent for the estate, reckoned that it would take forty years to transform the 2½ square miles from a mainly Victorian district to a modern estate, catering for 'the higher income groups'. The capital expenditure for the first ten years of the programme was calculated to be about £25 million. The Hagley Road, Bristol Road and Pershore Road sections which bound the estate were to be reconstructed as tree-lined boulevards. All but 70 acres of the estate, which extends in a wedge between the Hagley Road and Pershore Road from Five Ways almost to Harborne, was designed to be used for houses or flats. In line with the city's plan, housing density was increased, with the population estimated to rise from 8,000 to 26,000, involving the construction of 4,000 more homes. The 70 acres near Five Ways were zoned as a commercial centre, where new office blocks of between two and sixteen storeys in height were to be constructed. By March 1958 work had begun in demolishing houses in Westbourne Road.

In 1955 the Council defined fifteen Future Redevelopment Areas, effectively including the City's inner ring suburbs. Between 1955 and 1963 Birmingham cleared 12,347 houses in its redevelopment areas and 897 elsewhere. The 25-acre Lyndhurst Estate in Erdington was completed at a cost of £2 million, and work continued on the Millpool Hill Estate in King's Norton. On 15 October 1958 the Lord Mayor, Ald. D. Johnstone, opened the Hawkesley Farm Moat Estate. The three eight-storey blocks of flats were co-designed by the City Architect, A.G. Sheppard Fidler, and built by Wates Ltd. Small developments on existing or new sites continued apace throughout the remaining years of the decade. Three twelve-storey blocks of flats were built in the grounds of the former Fox Hollies Hall in Acocks Green, 300 dwellings, one of four storeys high, on a 15-acre site at Barnes Hill, California, were developed at a cost of £641,000, and 100 dwellings on a former pre-fab site at Gibbins Road in Selly Oak, were built for £213,000. Fifty-two four-storey blocks were constructed along Sheldon Heath Road, and seventy bungalows, houses and four-storey maisonettes were built on a 4-acre site at Quinton Hall. Other developments planned involved building in Bartley Green, Broadstone Road, Yardley, Manor Road, Witton, Park Hill, Hamstead, Quinton Road West, a bombed site in Rookery Road, Handsworth, Tower Hill, Perry Barr, World's End Lane, Quinton and Metchley Grange Estate, Harborne.

ten

Ring Roads, Bull Ring and Bright Shiny Stations

More than a decade after the end of the war, Birmingham city centre was still a drab, grey place. The Blitz had left ugly gaps in the street scene. Unsafe buildings were demolished or shored up, their frontages onto the road were covered in boards, and made uglier by fly-posting. There seemed a reluctance by companies to do anything about it and people made the best of what there was. The city needed a kick-start and this could only come from the City Council. A sequence of new initiatives eventually began the required redevelopment: important among these were the cutting of the Ring Road, the construction of the Bull Ring and the refurbishment of New Street Station. The construction of new road links, not least 'Spaghetti Junction', brought Birmingham well and truly into the second half of the twentieth century and back into the public limelight.

As in all things, there were downsides. In the process, redevelopment turned 1960s Birmingham into one vast building site. It was a miserable time picking one's way across the development sites, and there was also a cost. Some old familiar buildings were cleared away with reckless abandon, and roads were diverted, or lost completely. The City Engineer and Surveyor, Sir Herbert Manzoni, cared little for the past. Buildings, he believed, should have a built-in redundancy, to last no more than fifteen or twenty years. Many fine old buildings were demolished in the drive to build something more modern in their place. Manzoni constructed an efficient and functional city. There can be nothing but praise for his part in the clearance of the city's slums, but the city centre became altogether different, one designed by an engineer, rather than an architect. Many felt it proved to be a triumph of brutalism over aesthetics.

As early as 1918 city planners considered the need for an inner ring road as a means of dealing with traffic in the city centre. In 1939 plans were prepared for

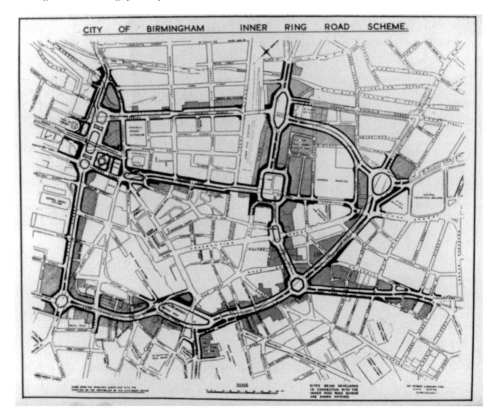

Manzoni's Inner Ring Road.

consideration, but the war forestalled any action. An advisory panel was set up and guidelines were prepared. Interested parties had an imput. The Chamber of Commerce, the Central Traders, the Council's Transport Department, the Chief Constable and the Architectural Association all gave evidence and advice regarding the scheme. The panel drew the following conclusions:

a. Traffic not having business in the city shopping centre should be diverted.

b. Vehicles having business in the centre should not be subject to restrictions but allowed to circulate freely – a one-way traffic system should be implemented.

c. The routes for public service vehicles should bring passengers to the heart of the city and within a reasonable distance of all parts of it. No one should have to walk more than 300 yards from an omnibus route.

d. The streets should be adapted to their purpose, e.g., busy shopping streets should not also be wide traffic arteries. Shopping streets should have wide footpaths to reduce dangers from traffic.

e. The spread of first-class shopping and commercial areas beyond the present limits should be encouraged.

In July 1943 the City Council approved in principle the layout of the Inner Ring Road around the city centre, and in so doing forgot a crucial principle of planning – plan for the future! What they agreed to was simply a modified version of the plan of 1918.

In 1944 the City Council approved the compulsory purchase of land required for the scheme at an estimated cost of £12,088,800, and the carrying out of the necessary road and sewer works, at a further estimated cost of £2.5 million. A Bill was presented to Parliament, and despite the post-war economic restraints, the Treasury gave loan sanction to the Council to purchase the land required for the scheme. Unfortunately, because of restrictions on new building, progress on the Inner Ring Road had to be deferred for ten years. In 1955, following a progressive build-up in traffic in the city centre over that decade, the scheme was reactivated. Construction of sections I and II, Suffolk Street to Carrs Lane and Upper Priory to Bath Street, were costed at £1,146,000. Approval was sought from the Minister of Transport and Civil Aviation to begin. Priority at the time though had been given to the construction of urban highways, but following a visit from the Minister, Harold Watkinson, permission was given on 18 January 1957 for the scheme to commence.

The initial scheme consisted of just under 4 miles of dual carriageway, encompassing Suffolk Street, Smallbrook Street, Worcester Street, Bell Street, Moor Street, Stafford Street, Loveday Street, a new section of road linking up to Bath Street, Great Charles Street and Easy Row. The circle was to be bisected by a widened Colmore Row and Upper Priory with a new section of road linking it to Moor Street. All roads were to be 110 feet wide, having two carriageways 38 feet wide with a central reservation 4 feet wide. The two footpaths were to be 15 feet wide. The width of road allowed for four lanes in each direction. Viaducts were planned where the new road crossed over old roads, and pedestrian underpasses were included at important road junctions. Construction of the Ring Road involved the compulsory purchase of more than 1,500 properties and the redevelopment of 80 acres of land, including 14 already in Corporation ownership. When complete, some 45 acres of land alongside the new road became available for developers.

The first section of the Ring Road, running from Suffolk Street along Smallbrook Ringway (as it was to be renamed), to Queen's Drive, was opened by the Minister for Transport, Ernest Marples, on 11 March 1960. It had cost £1,160,000. The next section completed lay between the Bull Ring and Carrs Lane, and by 1964 the bisecting road linking Moor Street, along Lower Priory to Snow Hill, was completed. The last link, completed on 30 December 1970, was the viaduct section in Suffolk Street. The following Sunday the eastern side of Suffolk Street Ringway was opened to two-way traffic leading into the twin 750 feet tunnels under Paradise Circus, emerging in Great Charles Street. The queen officially opened the Inner Ring Road on 7 April 1971, renaming it Queensway. It had been the intention that only the tunnels and their approaches should be known as Queensway, the remainder of the scheme was to be called the Ringway. However, in her speech, the

The cutting of Smallbrook Queensway, 1960.

The completed Smallbrook Queensway.The completed Smallbrook Queensway, 1964.

queen referred to the whole ring road as Queensway, and Queensway it became. The final cost was £35 million.

While traffic flowed more freely, which no one could deny, the city centre was now ringed by a concrete collar. The fifth resolution of the original concept, to extend the first class shopping and commercial area, went by the board. The area beyond the collar became a dead zone. The city centre was reduced to its 1731 limits. The underpasses, designed to protect pedestrians, were very difficult to negotiate, especially for pushchair and wheelchair users, having only stairs, as in the case of the underpass leading down to the Bull Ring from New Street and High Street. They became bleak and litter-strewn places and, for many, areas to be avoided at night.

The reconstruction of much of the commercial centre of Birmingham followed on piece-meal, along the new ring road. It began with the sporadic building of office blocks here and there, followed by larger and larger buildings, culminating in the building of the Bull Ring Centre. This complex included a multi-storey shopping precinct (costing £8 million and consisting of 350,000 square feet of shopping space), the city retail market, parking for 500 cars, a seven-storey office block, eight restaurants, four public houses, twenty-one escalators and an underground bus station, designed to handle 18 million passengers a year. In 1958 the City Council offered the Bull Ring area for redevelopment, and a local developer, J.L.G. Investments Ltd, and architect James A. Roberts, drew up plans for its development. Negotiations broke down over finance, and the city advertised the development, inviting outside companies to submit their plans. John Laing & Son's offer was eventually accepted. They appointed architects Sydney Greenwood and T.J. Hirst to design the centre, and sent Greenwood to America to see what lessons could be learnt. Work began in the summer of 1961, with John Laing Construction acting as the main contractor, with engineering construction and services by B.H. Broadbent. Mechanical and electrical services were organised by Oscar Faber & Partners, and Wakesman Trower & Partners were the quantity surveyors. The Duke of Edinburgh opened the completed Bull Ring Centre on 29 May 1964. The centre, at that time, was the most advanced development of its kind in the world and attracted international attention. Opened in the same year was James A. Roberts' iconic, twenty-five-storey Rotunda building which towered over the Bull Ring and immediately became a popular new landmark.

Also under construction at the time was the Ladywell Centre, an 11½-acre site designed by John Madin. Built on the Gooch Estate at a cost of £4 million, it was a continuation of the Bull Ring complex, along Bromsgrove and Pershore Streets, and included 100 shops, nightclubs, a cinema, dance hall, ice rink and a thirty-two-lane bowling alley. In addition 105 flats and maisonettes were also provided. Associated with the Ladywell scheme was the development of a new 27-acre multistorey wholesale market, built on an adjoining section of the Gooch Estate. It was a large complex; the original cost of construction was estimated at £9 million. The site was bounded by Bradford Street, skirting the old abattoir, along to Sherlock Street, Pershore Street, Bromsgrove Street, Dean Street, Gloucester Street and Edgbaston

The Aston Expressway in 1972. It cut a swathe through some of the city's worst slums.

Street to St Martin's Lane. In the process Jamaica Row was built over. The new market was to include meat, fish, poultry, fruit and vegetable markets. A revised plan was approved by the Council in 1969, and was submitted for approval to the Ministry of Housing and Local Government. Following a public enquiry in February 1970, the Ministry approved the scheme in July 1970, subject to a slight amendment to the boundaries. There were costly delays, and design work was halted as the planners negotiated with the Wholesalers' Association regarding the layout of the new market. A final agreement was reached which changed the original design from a two-storey building to one that was basically a single storey with perimeter offices at first floor level. The first phase of development, the building of the Meat, Poultry and Fish Market, was begun in October 1972. It was completed in 1974, just six weeks behind schedule, and opened on 17 February by the Lord Mayor, Cllr Mrs Marjorie Brown. The final bill was in excess of £14 million. Shortly after work had begun on the Wholesale Market, on the 30 November 1972 a new outdoor market was opened in Birmingham, the first in over 800 years. It was established under licence by Landval Markets Ltd, in Corporation Square. The sixty-five-stall market brought new life to a dead area of the city, situated between Corporation Street and Dale End.

The redevelopment of New Street Station was part of British Railway's London, Midland Region plan for the updating and electrification of the West Coast line, linking Euston, Birmingham, Manchester and Liverpool. It also dovetailed into the city's redevelopment programme for the Bull Ring and Smallbrook Queensway. In the process the entrance to the station was moved from Stephenson Street to the Ring Road, relieving traffic congestion from the New Street area. The plan for the new station made it a 'closed' station, with the building of a car park, refreshment rooms and offices immediately above the platforms and railway track, making it an underground station in fact. Work began on rebuilding in 1964, almost exactly 110 years after its original opening. Queen's Drive, and the Queen's Hotel, the original entrance to the station, were removed and covered by extra track and platforms. Over 200 columns, resting on piles driven down 30 feet below ground level, were erected to support a pre-stressed concrete roof above the track. The main contractors were C. Bryant & Son. All amenities, ticket office, refreshment rooms, bookstalls and toilets were at ground level. In addition a twenty-one-storey block of flats, Stephenson House, was erected over the station. Reopening occurred with the reconstruction of each platform, the whole being opened officially on 6 March 1967, at a cost of £4.5 million. The deck to support the tower block cost £93,000 and the shopping mall, consisting of some ninety-four shops, a further £6 million. A new corrugated concrete signal box, now statutorily listed, was opened on 3 July 1966.

The Gravelly Hill Multi-Level Interchange, Junction 6 of the M6, but better known to most as Spaghetti Junction, is one of the greatest engineering feats of the second half of the twentieth century. Its actual length is 0.6 of a mile long, with 2½ miles of connecting roads. It cost £8,170,000 to build. The junction was first mooted back in 1959 as an urban motorway linking the M1 and the M6. Initial plans consisted of an elevated roundabout serving the existing roads, constructed above the newly built motorway link, and with access roads joining the motorway.

In 1962 the Council proposed the cutting of the Aston Expressway to link the city with the motorway network; the first of four proposed motorway links, including Perry Barr, Quinton and Woodgate Valley links, the Rubery Bypass and

The construction of Spaghetti Junction, 1971.

the Coventry Road Expressway. In May 1963 revised plans were drawn up relating to the costed £6 million Expressway of six lanes. Because of a large number of shops and industrial premises along the old Aston and Lichfield Roads, it was decided to re-route it slightly, so that it would pass through an area of slum housing designated for demolition. The £7.1 million contract to construct the Expressway was won by two firms, R.M. Douglas Construction and Taylor Woodrow. Work on the Douglas section of the road, from Lancaster Circus to Tower Road, was begun on 6 January 1969. Taylor Woodrow, building the Tower Road to Gravelly Hill section, began three months earlier in September 1968. Work on the entire roadway was completed sixteen months ahead of schedule, and the Aston Expressway was opened on 1 May 1972.

Meanwhile there were delays in producing plans for the construction of the Gravelly Hill Interchange, due to the nature of the terrain, including a built-up area, a canal network and the river Tame. Eventually on 1 June 1965 the Ministry of Transport gave the go-ahead for work to begin. The project as it then stood was for an 80-feet high eight-level traffic network, costing £100 million. It was to be another three years though before work got underway. With a starting date of May 1968, Salford Reservoir was drained in the summer of 1967, as a prelude to diverting the channel of the river Tame, which was accomplished at a cost of £500,000. The firm of Monk & Co. of Lancashire constructed the Interchange. They used 167,000 cubic yards of concrete, 13,000 tons of reinforced steel and 425,000 supporting piles. The final cost, including land, and all other charges was £115 million. This important hub of the nation's motorways, linking the M1, M5 and M6, was opened on Wednesday 24 May 1972 by the Secretary of State for the Environment, Peter Walker. Roy Smith first coined its popular name of 'Spaghetti Junction' in an article for the *Birmingham Post* on 21 August 1968.

eleven

The Last of the Estates

The last of the major housing developments by the city occurred in the 1960s, culminating in the construction of the Druids Heath, Bromford Bridge, and Castle Vale Estates, and over the border in Warwickshire, at Chelmsley Wood. In the early 1960s the Council signed a series of small contracts with developers worth £3.5 million. The largest of these was with the firm of George Stubbings Ltd, for 337 dwellings, mainly houses, on the Ivy House Farm Estate in King's Heath; a deal worth £963,244. George Wimpey & Co. signed a second contract for 300 houses on land formerly owned by Rubery Hill Hospital on Bristol Road South, for a figure of £869,175. A third contract was negotiated for the construction of just fifty-one homes in the Queen's Road Scheme in Aston, by Alfred Langley Ltd., for £173,221. Morris & Jacombs Ltd's bid was accepted for the erection of three thirteen-storey blocks of flats, and fifty houses on the Pool Farm Estate at King's Norton, and Bryant & Son agreed to build 205 dwellings on the planned Castle Vale Estate, a deal worth £665,163. In addition they agreed to erect a block of forty-two flats and a primary school for a further £160,932.

In 1964 Birmingham purchased part of the Monyhull Hospital Estate, and combined with a former pre-fab site, had sufficient land to build dwellings for 2,000 families, creating a new community of nearly 8,000 people. Bryant & Son Ltd was commissioned to develop what was to become the Druids Heath Estate. Miall Rhys-Davies designed the estate under the direction of the City Architect, J.R. Sheriden-Sheddon. The area covered was 120 acres, bisected by Bells Lane, effectively creating two estates, each served by a small group of shops. The type of dwellings ranged from one-person bungalows to seven-person houses. Bryants developed on an industrial scale, using the Bison Wall Frame systems. They erected thirteen-storey blocks of fifty flats over a period of nine weeks, using eleven men

Druids Heath Estate

Schedule of Accommodation

Bison Wall Frame

	Number of Homes	*Number of Persons*
Sixteen 13-storey blocks, 1-bedroom	416	832
2-bedroom	384	1536

Bryant Low-Rise

3-bedroom five person homes	603	3,015
3-bedroom four person homes	38	152
2-bedroom four person mews flats	168	672
4-bedroom seven person homes	75	525
1-bedroom aged person bungalows	105	210

Traditional

4-storey maisonettes	88	391
3-bedroom five person homes	38	190
4-bedroom seven person homes	40	280
Dwellings attached to shops	10	50
	1,965	7,853

per block. Their three-bedroom houses, using pre-cast techniques, were put up in twenty-five man-weeks as opposed to the traditional method of forty man-weeks. The company was supplied from its own factory at Handsworth, established in 1964. Once the factory was up and running, production leapt from eight to thirty-six houses per week.

Richard Crossman, Minister of Housing and Local Government, performed the official opening ceremony of the estate on 3 December 1965.

At the end of 1964 the City Council authorised the purchase of the old racecourse at Bromford Bridge. City Architect, J.R. Sheriden-Shedden, and the City Engineer and Surveyor, drew up a master plan for its development. In January 1965 the plan, for the building of 1,750 homes on the estate, was approved. One of the main features of the development of Bromford Bridge was a curved spine road, running from east to west. The estate, intending to house 6,000 people, was of mixed medium and high-density housing. A group of five thirteen-storey blocks of flats were built on the eastern sector of the estate, below the estate's spinal road,

Bromford Drive. Beyond them were two more twenty-storey blocks and similar ones near the Chester Road. Despite these intrusive blocks, more than two thirds of the estate was finally built as two-storey houses. More than 200 houses were also built by the private sector for sale. A 10-acre shopping centre was proposed at the corner of Chester Road and Kingsbury Road, to serve Bromford Bridge and the adjoining Castle Vale Estate. In addition a number of more local shops also featured in the City Architect's plan. Tame Valley Primary School was built to serve the needs of the younger children of the estate. On the north side of Bromford Bridge, a wide area of open space, at no point less than 80 yards, was intended to be left as a shield from the then proposed M6, which was cut between the estate and the river Tame to the north. In the end, due to pressure on space, Cameronian Croft, Chillinghome Road, Wanderer Walk and Berrandale Road, butted right up to the motorway.

In 1959 the city purchased the former Castle Bromwich Airfield site with a view to developing it as a housing estate. It was to be the last major municipal estate built in Birmingham. Planning of the estate was controversial, leading to factionalism within the Council. The House Building Committee and the Architects Department put forward a proposal for a garden city development, housing 15,000 people. The Public Works Committee and City Engineers Department favoured a more industrial approach, housing 22,000 people. The industrial approach of prefabricated system-built high-rise buildings attracted Government subsidy, and as a matter of course was favoured by the building industry. One of the main systems was the 'Bison' system, developed by Concrete Ltd and adopted by Bryants Ltd. This company was eventually to win the contract to build the Castle Vale Estate, using George Stubbings & Co. as a major subcontractor.

Castle Vale was planned as a development of 5,000 dwellings with thirty-four tower blocks mostly in two spines running the length of the estate. The layout was austere and geometric – a throwback to the 1930s, or even to the Stalinist estates of Eastern Europe. It was an engineer's concept totally lacking in concern for the intended inhabitants. At ground level the estate was open and windswept. In wet weather the area became a quagmire. There was no infrastructure. Shops and other civic amenities only came later, as an afterthought. Industrialised methods were used in their construction too. The shops, single-storied, were functional but plain. It could have been different, with a little thought, and some generous planting of mature trees and shrubs. In 1993 the estate was taken over by a Housing Action Trust, and gradually the old tower blocks were demolished, to be replaced by new low-rise houses built on a more human scale.

As late as 1972 there were still some 14,000 dwellings in Birmingham that were classed as slums. The city looked once more beyond its boundaries. In 1963 planning permission was given by Warwickshire County Council for Birmingham to develop an estate for 50,000 people at Chelmsley Wood. In addition, opposition was eventually also overcome in North Worcestershire, and approval was given in 1969 to the building of 11,000 houses at Frankley, Rubery and Hawkesley.

The Castle Vale Estate, 1970 – a soul-less housing development, now being rebuilt on a more human scale.

Here in North Worcestershire particularly, landscape architecture was to play a major role in housing development. Houses were fitted into the landscape, rather than shaping the landscape to suit the housing. Trees and hedges were kept, and houses were integrated amongst them. As a consequence roads gently curved, and houses were built in clusters to foster a community spirit amongst neighbours. The city had been a long time learning what George Cadbury had advocated a hundred years ago.

twelve

Revitalising the City

The Local Government Act of 1972 established new local government areas throughout England and Wales. The Metropolitan District of Birmingham was established as part of the Metropolitan County of West Midlands. It comprised the existing thirty-nine wards of the old city, plus three new wards in the ceded Royal Borough of Sutton Coldfield. Solihull, originally intended to be absorbed into the city, remained independent, having Chelmsley Wood and Castle Bromwich ceded to it, to make it a viable entity with a population of 75,000.

Sutton Coldfield comprises an area of 5,549 hectares, of which 900 hectares include Sutton Park, and another 1,500 its green belt. This is roughly 21% of the total acreage of the post-1974 City of Birmingham. Its three new wards were Four Oaks, New Hall and Vesey. Four Oaks is made up of Four Oaks, Little Sutton, Reddicap Heath and Mere Green, including an extensive area of Sutton Park and the Green Belt. New Hall Ward contains Falcon Lodge, Minworth, Reddicap Heath, Walmley and part of Whitehouse Common. The town centre also lies within this ward. The third ward, Vesey, is situated south of the town centre, and includes Boldmere, parts of New Oscott and Walmley, Wylde Green and part of Sutton Park.

Within Birmingham itself, in that same year of 1974 the Council announced a moratorium on redevelopment within the city centre until a master plan had been approved. The demolition of Galloway's Corner at the junction of Colmore Row and New Street in 1970 led to a commercial decline in the area, leaving a site, though grassed, looking decidedly unfinished. Pedestrianisation had been introduced in 1972-73, a step generally applauded by most people, and development shifted towards the proposed 1930s Civic Centre with the opening of the new Repertory Theatre in 1971 and the new Central Library in 1974.

Broad Street had never been an entity in its own right, like New Street, Corporation Street or the High Street. Instead it was a means of access between the town centre and Five Ways. The new development of the Calthorpe Estate at Five Ways, and the construction of the Central Library, Repertory Theatre and Alpha Tower, all emphasised the neglect that was Broad Street. The completion of the Paradise Circus scheme by Henry Boot plc. in the 1980s, which included roofing over the Central Library and enclosing it in glass, an extension to the School of Music, a new concert hall, a small exhibition hall, the construction of the Copthorne Hotel (opened in 1987), and facing it, Chamberlain House office block, but more importantly a pedestrian bridge over the ring road to the Hall of Memory, paved the way for the development of Broad Street. In 1983 proposals were put forward by the city to build an International Convention Centre in Broad Street. Total cost of the centre was put at £121 million; £40 million of which was sought from, and provided by, a grant from the European Community.

As work got underway clearing the site in late 1986, an Urban Development Agency for East Birmingham was established soon after, to rejuvenate some 2,300 acres of the old industrial city. This was a joint venture between the Council and private enterprise, including five construction companies, Bryant, Douglas, Galliford, Tarmac and Wimpey. The Heartlands development was centred on Aston, Nechells, Duddeston, Bordesley and Bromford. It was intended to create up to 30,000 new jobs within a ten-year period, at an estimated development cost of £1 billion. Two aspects of the scheme were the development of Waterlinks, a mixed development of business, industry and housing, based around the existing canal network, and Bordesley Village, a new residential area at the southern end of the development.

The International Convention Centre (ICC) was opened in 1990. It was designed to, and in fact has, attracted national and multi-national conferences. It has eleven main halls, of which five can be sub-divided for smaller meetings. There are two large halls, one primarily for musical concerts, and seats 2,200; the other for conferences, and seats 1,500. Since its opening the ICC has played host to the G8 Conference, which included the former US President, Bill Clinton, the International Lions and the annual CBI Conferences. The construction of the ICC was the start of a more intensive development of the Broad Street area. The canal system off Gas Street was opened up to tourism by the demolition of a number of buildings along Broad Street, and the conversion or rebuild of those canal-side warehouses and small offices into restaurants, cafes and public houses. Immediately opposite the ICC was built the Hyatt Regency International Hotel, and further down Broad Street, a second new hotel, the Novotel. Over the following decade a number of public houses and clubs sprang up, including the conversion of the eighteenth-century Brasshouse, making Broad Street a popular entertainment area. Adjoining the ICC is the National Indoor Arena, built as a joint venture between the City Council and the Sports Council. It was part of a £200 million private development at Brindley Place, a 26-acre complex, housing hotels, offices, the National Aquarium, cinemas, a covered shopping area and public houses built on or around the existing canal

The building of the ICC marked the opening of the Broad Street area.

system. Linking the pedestrian walk from the Central Library, across the Ring Road to the ICC, was constructed a paved area, which, marking the 100th anniversary of Birmingham as a city, was named Centenary Square.

This modern renaissance of Birmingham now extended eastward into Digbeth and north-eastwards to include Aston University; an area renamed Eastside. It is an extensive area, 420 acres, bounded by Digbeth and Deritend High Street, the Coventry Road, Watery Lane, Lawley and Dartmouth Middleway, Aston Road North and the end of Corporation Street to Lancaster Circus, James Watt and Moor Street Queensway back to the Bull Ring and Digbeth. Development started with the construction of Millenium Point in Curzon Street, a new science museum opened in September 2001 at a cost of £114 million.

The main stumbling block to the development of Eastside was the mental and physical barrier created by the Inner Ring Road. As a consequence the 'Concrete Collar', as it had became known, was broken at Masshouse Circus, as a gateway to the intended development. The elevated section along Moor Street was removed and new roads cut, creating not an improvement, but a complicated section of sub-divided roadway. On the positive side this part of Birmingham is to become the intellectual area of the city. Key features of Eastside are the intended construction of a new Central Library, a feasibility study of which has already been undertaken by the Richard Rogers Partnership. A completion date of 2010 has been given. There is also to be a Media Village along the canal at Warwick Bar, a proposed new

The new Bull Ring and St Martin's church, the very heartbeat of the city.

Matthew Boulton College fronting Jennens Road, accommodating 15,000 students and due to open in September 2005, and a technology based business park straddling the Digbeth Branch Canal. In addition a shopping development is to be built to serve the area. The Martineau Galleries is to consist of 1.2 million square foot retail development. A new 9-acre city centre park is to be laid out, but already it has run into controversy as to whether it will be designed as some geometric plan, or be a more traditional and restful open space with grass and trees. The new development is expected to take ten years. As at February 2002, the total cost for the creation of Eastside was £6 billion.

In November 2002 plans were revealed for the development of Masshouse, which will link the existing city to the proposed Eastside site. The London based firm of Edward Cullinan Architects, in association with Acdas AHR Architects Ltd, drew up the plans. The chosen developers are David McLean Developments. The scheme will include 500,000 square feet of offices, 550 apartments, a 350-bed hotel, cafes bars, restaurants and shops.

As plans were drawn up for Eastside, work began on the redevelopment of the Bull Ring. Taking three years to build, the developers of the new Bull Ring were Birmingham Alliance. An investment of over £1 billion provided 110,000 square metres of retail accommodation on three levels. The Bull Ring, which opened in September 2003, became home to 146 shops, fifty-seven of them new to the city. The two major stores are Debenhams and Selfridges.

The Selfridges building defies architectural classification, and as such is singled out. It could be described as a huge slug in sequins. Designed by Future Systems, it is four storeys high, and 15,000 aluminium discs, mounted onto a blue surface area, cover its outer skin. At night when lit, it has an eerie beauty. In its positioning the Selfridges building clashes with the real focal point of the Bull Ring – St Martin's church. The store is also unbalanced against the other side of the crescent that almost, but not quite, surrounds the parish church. The Selfridges store is a unique building that no doubt will come to represent Birmingham in the same way that the Rotunda once did. It looks out of place in its surroundings though, a unique building sitting in a crescent of mundane architecture. What has happened in this redevelopment, and happened by happy chance, is that the restored St Martin's has reasserted itself as the primary architectural structure in the Bull Ring. The removal of the concrete collar at St Martin's Circus has once again opened up the view from the junction of New Street and High Street. It is St Martin's church that stands out.

Birmingham's landscape history has once again turned full circle. The heart of the city has returned to its original focal point. The failure of the 1960s, the constricting Inner Ring Road, is being removed, thus opening up the city centre to expansion. The development of the Convention Centre District has been invigorating, as indeed will be the development of Eastside. The proposed Central Park here will give the scheme a human dimension. What the future planners of the city must always consider is whom they are designing for. Cities are first and foremost, for people.

End Notes

Chapter one

1. *Victoria County History, Warwickshire,* vol. 1, 1964, p.332.
2. *Cartae Antiquae* (Chancery) T.41 P.R.O. "Thol" mentioned in the charter, was the toll levied on stallholders and traders at the market. At the time the toll was:1d. for every horse, ½d for every ox, 1d for every five sheep bought or sold at the market.
3. Close Roll (Chancery) 35 Henry III, p.633.
4. *Warwickshire Feet of Fines*, Dugdale Society vol. 2, No. 479.
5. *The Big Fire of the Town of Birmingham*, Razi, Z., Birmingham and Warwicks. Arch. Soc. Trans., vol. 88, 1976-7.
6. *Antiquities of Warwickshire*, Dugdale, Sir William, 1656, p.660.
7. Birmingham Reference Library, Archives. Hereafter BRL Deed 120835.
8. *English Historical Review*, XXXI, p.603.
9. *English Guilds*, Smith, Toulmin, 1870, p.249.
10. *Leland*, second edition by Thomas Hearne, Oxford, 1745, vol. IV, p.108.
11. Indenture of Lease, BRL 249974.
12. Foley MSS FV1/MB fl. Hereford Record Office.
13. Probate Inventory. P.R.O.
14. *Victoria County History, Warwickshire,* vol. II, 1964, p.195.
15. *Discourses of the Navy,* Holland, John, Navy Record Society, 1896, p.243.
16. *A New Voyage to Italy,* 1695.
17. BRL 181614.
18. BRL181678.
19. BRL 252605.
20. BRL 181870.
21. BRL 324166.

Chapter two

1. BRL 181756.
2. BRL 252666.
3. BRL 249987.
4. *St Philip's Cathedral, Memorandums and Agreements of the Commissioners*, BRL Archives Dept.

Chapter three

1. *An History of Birmingham*, William Hutton, 1780, p.79.
2. An Act for building two new chapels in Birmingham. 12 Geo. III, c.64.
3. BRL 28425, 284279, 284276.
4. BRL 181794.
5. BRL 270065.
6. *An History of Birmingham*, William Hutton, 1780, p.48.
7. BRL 276529.
8. *Old and New Birmingham,* Dent, R.K., 1880, p.208, and *The Making of Birmingham*, Dent, R.K., 1894, p.227.
9. *Provincial Towns of Georgian England*, Chalkin, C.W., 1974, p.85.
10. BRL 276630.
11. BRL 324353.
12. BRL 453531.
13. *A Century of Birmingham Life,* vol. II, Langford, J. A., p.6.
14. Proposals with the Plan & Specification for building the Crescent in Birmingham by C. Norton, Builder. 1795. (BRL).

Chapter four

1. *Reminiscences of a Gentlewoman of the Last Century*, Beale, Catherine Hutton, Cornish Brothers, Birmingham, 1891, p.193.

Bibliography

Primary Sources

Chubb, Leonard, *Calendar of Deeds,* 1913. Local Studies Dept., Central Library,
    Birmingham.
Collection of Deeds. Archives Dept., Central Library, Birmingham.
Sales Catalogue Collection 1798-1970, Local Studies Dept., Central Library, Birmingham.

Books and Periodicals

Beale, Catherine Hutton, *Reminiscences of a Gentlewoman of the Last Century*, Cornish Bros,
    Birmingham, 1891.
Birmingham (Central Development) Compulsory Purchase Order, 1946.
Birmingham Plan 1973, 1993, 2000, 2001.
Bournville Village Trust 1900-1955, BVT Publications, 1955.
Briggs, Asa, *History of Birmingham vol. 2*, Birmingham City Council, 1952.
Brindley Place, Birmingham. Brindleyplace plc, (undated).
Bunce, Vince, *et al., History of the Corporation of Birmingham, 1885-1940.*
Cadbury, George jr., *Town Planning with special reference to the Birmingham Schemes,*
    Longmans, Green & Co., 1915.
Cannadine, David, *Lords and Landlords – the Aristocracy of Towns,* Leicester University Press,
    1980.
Chalklin, C.W., *The Provincial Towns of Georgian England,* Montreal, 1974.
Chinn, Carl, *Homes for People,* Birmingham Books, 1991.
City of Birmingham, Druids Heath Development, 1965.
City of Birmingham Handbook, 1928-1965.
City of Birmingham Housing Committee Reports, 1901-7.
City of Birmingham Inner Ring Road Scheme, City of Birmingham Public Works Committee,
    1957.
Dent, R.K., *Old and New Birmingham*, Birmingham, 1880, *Making of Birmingham,*
    Birmingham, 1894.

Developing Birmingham – 100 years of City Planning. Birmingham City Council Development Dept., 1989.

Dugdale, Sir William. *Antiquities of Warwickshire,* 1656.

Dugdale Society No. 2., Feet of Fines.

Eastside: Design and Movement Framework 2003. Birmingham City Council.

English Historical Review, XXXI.

Gerrard, A.J., and Slater, T.R., *Managing a Conurbation – Birmingham & its Region*, Brewin Books, 1996.

Gill, Conrad, *History of Birmingham, vol. 1*. Birmingham City Council, 1952.

Harborne Tenants Ltd, Prospectus, 1908, Reports & Accounts, 1908-1947.

Heartlands – Annual Reports and Accounts, 1993-94, 1994-95. Birmingham Heartlands Development Corporation.

Holly Bank Village (Prospectus) Mutual Housings Ltd, 1924.

Hutton, William, *An History of Birmingham*, Birmingham, 1780.

Langford, J.A., *A Century of Birmingham Life*. Birmingham, 1879.

Llewelyn-Davies *et al.*, *Inner Area Study*, 1976, 1979, 1981.

Manzoni, Herbert J., *The production of Fifty Thousand Municipal Houses*, City of Birmingham, 1939.

Navy Record Society, 1896.

Nettlefold, J.S., *Slum Reform and Town Planning,* 1907, *Practical Housing*. Garden City Press., Letchworth, 1908.

The Official Opening of Hawkesley Farm Moat Estate, 1958.

Planning and Building Control. Birmingham City Council Planning Dept., 1977.

Proposals with the Plans and Specification for building the Crescent in Birmingham by C. Norton, Builder, 1795.

Razi, Z., *The Big Fire of the Town of Birmingham*. Birmingham and Warwickshire Archaeological Society, vol. 88, 1976-77.

Report of the Artizans Dwelling Committee, 1884, Birmingham Corporation.

Smith, R.J., *The Changing Housing Environment: Birmingham 1931-1967*. Research Paper No. 14, History of Birmingham Project, School of History, Birmingham University.

Smith, Toulmin, *English Guilds*, 1870.

Snape, John, *Estates in the Parish of Birmingham – The property of Sir Thomas,* Gooch. 1796.

Sutcliffe, S., and Smith, R.J., *History of Birmingham vol. 3*. Birmingham City Council, 1970.

Victoria County History of Warwickshire, vols I, II & VII, 1964.

Water's Edge at Brindley Place. Golley Slater Brooker, Birmingham, (undated).

When We Build Again, Bournville Village Trust, George Allen & Unwin, 1941.

Newscuttings and Magazines

Birmingham Central Library, Local Studies Dept categories:
Brindley Place 1980-1995
Bull Ring 1956-2004
Eastside 2001-2004
German War 1939-1945
Housing 1914-1980
Railways 1963-1968
Streets 1914-2000
Modern House and Home, 1937-39.

Index